LONNIE FRISBEE
CATALYST FOR REVIVAL

LONNIE FRISBEE

CATALYST FOR REVIVAL

The New Move of the Holy Spirit, from Hippies to Homosexuals

LEE ALLEN HOWARD

Acceptable Books
Jamestown, NY

Scripture References

LONNIE FRISBEE, CATALYST FOR REVIVAL: THE NEW MOVE OF THE HOLY SPIRIT, FROM HIPPIES TO HOMOSEXUALS

"Lonnie was so controversial that legends abound; the truth needs to be discerned from myth."
—DAVID DI SABATINO

"But God chose the foolish things of this world to put the wise to shame. He chose the weak things of this world to put the powerful to shame. What the world thinks is worthless, useless, and nothing at all is what God has used to destroy what the world considers important."
—1 CORINTHIANS 1:27–28 CEV

"The Lord is my shepherd, and he knows I'm gay."
—REV. TROY D. PERRY

Contents

1.   Who Was Lonnie Frisbee?

Have you heard of Lonnie Frisbee? With all my studies of Pentecostal and charismatic church history over the past three decades, I should have but didn't. If it weren't for a recent documentary about his life, I never would have learned about him—and perhaps neither would you.

Thanks to filmmaker David Di Sabatino's *Frisbee: The Life and Death of a Hippie Preacher* (2006), the influence of a 1960s flower child has taken its rightful place in the annals of the twentieth-century outpouring of the Holy Spirit. Di Sabatino's film, which he calls a "Bible story," sketches the life, ministry, and demise of a young man known elsewhere as "the original Jesus Freak[1]" (Di Sabatino, Frisbee).

In this book, which recounts Frisbee's life and provides the context in which he came to faith and entered ministry, I simply call him Lonnie. I gather together here all the published sources from those who knew or knew of Lonnie, and I let them speak in their own words.

---

1   The term "Jesus freak" was made popular in recent years through a *DC Talk* song. But the term "was originally used by the Jesus Movement as a means of turning the other cheek. They accepted the title that was meant to be an insult and made it their own." (Crowder)

Lonnie and the Jesus Movement

Under Lonnie's ministry, untold thousands were converted, healed, and filled with the Holy Spirit in a greater move of God sparked in the 1960s that kindled most of North America's revival in the past forty years. Youth minister Hardin Crowder claims, "Frisbee is seen by many as the match that lit the flame that was 'The Jesus Movement'" (Crowder).

Why would God use a man without higher education from a drugged-up, dropped-out generation to build his Kingdom? Because Lonnie loved God. And God used him as a catalyst for Holy Spirit revival.

Lonnie loved people, too, and men especially. This is one of the reasons you've never heard of him.

But now that I've learned about Lonnie Frisbee, I've grown to love him.

Let me tell you why.

2. Lonnie's Early Life

Lonnie Ray Frisbee was born to Ray Frisbee and Janette Ashley on June 6, 1949. His father was a full-blooded Native American, Cherokee and Choctaw, whose father was raised on a reservation (Frisbee and Sachs, Not By Might 17). Lonnie describes his childhood as "bizarre" and his father, a country-western entertainer, as "a honky-tonk singer with whiskey breath." His mother's family descended from a line of ministers that traces its roots to a revival in Essex, England (18).

At fifteen, Ray Frisbee married Janette, who was sixteen (19). They immediately started a family having, in addition to Lonnie, Stanley and Wesley (21).

Family troubles

Both Lonnie and his older brother were born with club feet. Lonnie had two major surgeries on his left leg to drop his Achilles tendon. Because of his frailties, Lonnie recalls that neighborhood kids bullied and beat him up, calling him and his brother "pigeon toe" (19). Lonnie says, "They were little children with big cruelties" (20).

Ray Frisbee, according to Lonnie, was a womanizer, an alcoholic, and a gambler (17–18). Ray was cruel and violent, often beating Janette and going on rampages where he would bust out windows and break the dishes (17). When Lonnie was about four years old, his father abandoned them (21).

Ray Frisbee never believed Lonnie was his child and acted accordingly. Lonnie states his mother was faithful, but his father, never. Ray refused to pay child support for Lonnie, claiming that he was the milkman's son (21). For a while, Lonnie and his brothers were raised by Janette alone.

Janette later married Lyle Graham, with whom she had Scottie and Stevie (23). Lyle Graham hated everything about Ray Frisbee and, says Lonnie, raised Ray's boys "in total rejection." Lonnie says of his step-father, "I wanted his approval in the beginning and was starving for affection, but never got it" (25). Lonnie grew to hate Graham also (24).

The abuse begins

During the time when Lonnie's mother and Lyle Graham were working out their respective divorces and their new marriage, they dropped off the Frisbee boys at a strange home (24). Lonnie reports:

> I just remember them taking us there, introducing us to these strangers, and leaving. And that's where we lived for a while. I don't even know how long it was. It was when some of the first abuse happened to me. An older boy stripped down a whole bunch of us children that were living there. We were forced to be in a doghouse naked, and there was some abuse that started to take place. (24)

When Lonnie was eight years old, his mother had a neighborhood teenager babysit the boys. Lonnie remembers,

> He was a high school senior, and he paid special attention to me. I really liked him, and he played games with us, and put me on his shoulders. It all seemed so innocent, and normal,

and fun. Sometimes he would put me on his lap, and read to me, and then I remember him stroking my hair (25).

At first it felt good for someone to show Lonnie any kind of personal attention and affection. But it turned into a nightmare because the young man took Lonnie into the shower with him. "He undressed us both," Lonnie reveals, "and in the shower sexually molested me" (25).

> After it was over he bound me to secrecy, but I was so traumatized that I finally got up enough courage to tell my mother. My parents subsequently had a meeting with the babysitter's parents, and the adults finally concluded that "Lonnie is making it all up." Unbelievably, in a short time, they even allowed this young pedophile to baby-sit us again. When he got me alone he said, "Lonnie, why did you say those things about me?" (25)

The young man allegedly threatened Lonnie and molested him repeatedly over the next few years. Lonnie was terrified to tell anyone, "filled with shame and guilt and confusion." Ultimately, nothing was done about it. A psychologist told him later that this abuse broke the foundations of his life (26).

Lonnie accepts Christ

However, not all was violent and dark during these years. Lonnie's maternal grandmother often took him to First Christian, a Pentecostal assembly where they spoke in tongues and shouted "Hallelujah!"

At a puppet show in Orange, California, he knelt and accepted Christ. He was active at church and especially enjoyed his summer stays at Camp Seely, which he never wanted to leave (26).

An artist, a dancer, and a gay young man

As a young teen, Lonnie studied art and won awards for his paintings. Matt Coker in his *OC Weekly* article, "The Original Jesus Freak," says, "He was always an excellent artist and something of a cut-up. He'd show up at Corona del Mar High School dances with his face painted half-black, half-white" (Coker, First Jesus Freak). Light and dark, inside and out.

Despite being born with a partial club foot, Lonnie loved to dance and in 1966 was featured on Casey Kasem's *Shebang*, a west-coast version of *American Bandstand*.[2] He also lettered in wrestling (Frisbee and Sachs 46). At fifteen, he ran away from home—"the same year he and a buddy entered into the underground gay scene in Laguna Beach" (Coker, First Jesus Freak).

At seventeen Lonnie dropped out of high school and, on a scholarship from the Boys Club of America, entered the Academy of Art in San Francisco, which put him right in the middle of the Haight-Ashbury district's 1967 "Summer of Love" (Frisbee and Sachs 44–45).

---

2   YouTube: https://youtu.be/LnsK4FyTlbw?t=44.

3. Hippie Trips Out on Jesus

Lonnie was preppy in high school. But after he moved to San Francisco, he says, "My pompadour morphed into extremely long hair, a full-length beard, beads, bells, long robes, and sandals. Let's not forget the flowers in my hair" (Frisbee and Sachs 44).

Historian of the Jesus Movement Larry Eskridge describes him this way: "Slight of build, long-haired, bearded, and often dressed in leather with small pouches hanging from his belt, he looked like a little teenage Jesus" (Eskridge 33).

In his autobiography, *Not By Might Nor By Power*, Lonnie paints himself as a "nudist vegetarian hippie."

A gay and psychedelic seeker

Di Sabatino reveals that in the Haight-Ashbury, "Frisbee was recruited by an older male figure into the gay lifestyle" (Jackson, Quest 388). Being gay, however, is not a lifestyle, but an orientation.[3]

Like many young people at the time, Lonnie embraced the psychedelic drug culture and embarked on a spiritual quest (Lonnie Frisbee: Wikipedia). He made occasional trips back to

---

3 "Sexual orientation is an enduring pattern of romantic or sexual attraction (or a combination of these) to persons of the opposite sex or gender, the same sex or gender, or to both sexes or more than one gender" (Sexual Orientation). See also http://www.glaad.org/reference/offensive.

southern California to "get nude and seek God" (Frisbee and Sachs 49). Coker picks up the story here.

> Frisbee was a natural-born leader who'd take small caravans of friends to Tahquitz Canyon outside Palm Springs, where everyone would smoke weed, get naked and drop acid. Like a lot of kids searching for meaning, Lonnie tried mysticism and the occult but found them unfulfilling. That led him to the Bible.

> During one Tahquitz Canyon excursion, after the usual turn-on/tune-in/drop-out ritual, Frisbee whipped out the Good Book and started reading the Gospel of John, the one about God not sending his Son into the world to condemn it, but to save it. By the time Frisbee was done, everyone was in tears. Lonnie led the tribe to Tahquitz Falls and baptized them. (Coker, First Jesus Freak)

Even before his conversion, we see the call of God on Lonnie's life and the power of the Holy Spirit manifesting during his evangelistic efforts, however confused they were doctrinally and morally. He was not finished seeking.

Christ calls Lonnie to ministry

One day in 1967 the seventeen-year-old trekked the wilderness alone. He found his favorite spot, shed his clothes, and screamed at heaven, "Jesus, if you are really real, reveal yourself to me!" He recalls that the atmosphere began to change, "to tingle, and shimmer, and glow." Lonnie was shocked and frightened (Frisbee and Sachs 50). He recounts,

I didn't hear an audible voice, but knew that I was in the presence of God Almighty. Then I saw a radiant vision clear as crystal. **I saw thousands and thousands of young people at the ocean, lined up in huge crowds along the coast—and they were going out into the water being baptized.** I could see it! I knew instantly that Jesus was real—and that He was calling me to follow Him. As the Lord lifted up my eyes I saw a harvest field of people. They were like a huge wheat field. I saw in the vision thousands and thousands of people in the valley of decision.

The power of the Holy Spirit surrounded me from within and from without. Then I saw a light from heaven come down and ordain me—and I could hear Him say, "Go in my name, for I have touched your lips with a coal of fire that burns ever before the presence of God." ... I came off that mountain a different person. (50–51, emphasis mine)

Lonnie said God "told him that he would have a unique ministry, and that he was not to be afraid" (Di Sabatino). Lonnie explains it this way: "[T]he Lord showed me that there was a light on me that He was placing on my life, and it was Jesus Christ, and I was going to go bear the word of the Lord" (Lonnie Frisbee: Mother's Day).

Di Sabatino remarks, "Whatever happened to Lonnie Frisbee in the canyon that day so transformed him that it shaped the course of his entire life" (Di Sabatino).

Christianity in 1960s counterculture

San Francisco, and especially the Haight-Ashbury district, had since the 1950s become "bohemian and Beat-friendly," according to Eskridge in *God's Forever Family*, "the first major outpost of this developing counterculture in late 1966 and during 67's famous Summer of Love" (Eskridge 12).

"Christianity was not something the revolutionary counterculture of the 60s was always often willing to embrace," explains Hardin Crowder. "Christianity was seen as the religion of 'the man' [the establishment] and the moral police who wanted to kill free love" (Crowder). Yet evangelism exploded in this environment and swept the west coast and the nation.

The Jesus People: Old-Time Religion in the Age of Aquarius reveals how Lonnie explained the rise of evangelistic ministries during this time:

> He suggests that the Six-Day War of June 1967 between Israel and the surrounding Arab nations set the stage for the last days before Christ's second coming. When Israel regained her long-lost territory, a prophecy was fulfilled that signaled the beginning of the end times. (Enroth, Ericson Jr. and Peters 12)

Lonnie believed a great end-time harvest was about to be ushered onto the world scene. Such dispensational premillennialism was a hallmark of the times, demonstrated by the popularity of Hal Lindsey's 1970 bestseller, *The Late Great Planet Earth*. "The doctrine of the pretribulation rapture," says Vineyard historian Bill Jackson, "became the eschatology of the Jesus Movement" (Jackson, Quest 32).

Let's take a step back to examine the influences that helped shape Lonnie into the man and minister he became.

4. Ted Wise, Lonnie's First Mentor

John MacDonald was a classmate of Billy Graham's (class of 1943) at Wheaton College in Illinois. After pastoring several churches in northern California, MacDonald was chosen in 1960 to pastor 200-member First Baptist Church of Mill Valley, just above San Francisco across the Golden Gate Bridge (Eskridge 12).

Elizabeth and Ted Wise

Late in 1964 Elizabeth Wise began attending MacDonald's church. Raised Baptist, she had professed faith at age eleven. Now a young woman, Liz had married and, unknown to the conservative church members, often attended Sunday morning service while coming down from the previous evening's acid trip. Eventually she asked the church to pray for her husband Ted (12).

Warren "Ted" Wise was a native of Lakeport, California, who had joined the Navy in the mid-1950s and then taken work as a sail-maker. Always fascinated with drug use, he experimented with marijuana and heroin. He was interested in art and poetry and, at Sierra College, met Liz. She relocated to San Francisco in 1959, followed shortly thereafter by Ted. They joined "a Beat commune on O'Farrell Street in the city's North Beach bohemian enclave. 'Our basic identity,' Wise recalled, 'was as beatniks'" (12–13).

11

Both Liz and Ted tried LSD and loved it; tripping became routine. It was a wild life in more ways than one. Ted admitted he caroused with other women, leaving his wife and their two children at home. That's when Liz started attending First Baptist and came home "glowing" (14). She worked on evangelizing her husband.

Eventually, Ted read the New Testament and became enamored with Jesus. Convinced of his own sin and of Christ's divinity, Ted cried out to God to save him. The result? "Jesus knocked me off my metaphysical ass," he says. "I could choose Him or literally suffer a fate worse than death" (14–15).

Pastor MacDonald baptized Ted, who not only participated in church but invited his counterculture friends. The new visitors didn't go over well with the conservative older members. MacDonald estimates that about "half of his original congregation eventually left the church because of the hip newcomers" (17).

Birth of the Christian commune

Ted and Liz Wise became close friends with three other couples who, by late 1966, "had begun to form the nucleus of a Bay Area group of bohemian evangelical Christians." These couples were Jim and Judy Doop, Steve and Sandi Heefner, and Dan and Sandy Sands. After participating in Golden Gate Park's January 1967 "Human Be-in," the four couples toyed with the idea of forming a Christian commune. According to Ted, they agreed that they "ought to live out the Book of Acts like a script" (19–22).

Ted presented to church members his concerns for beatniks and the influx of seekers to San Francisco but concluded,

"[I]t was obvious that MacDonald and the people of First Baptist simply did not care about the hippies and were not willing to help them." However, he convinced Pastor MacDonald to tour the district with him. While doing so, MacDonald realized he was a "square," but Ted had "remarkable rapport" everywhere he went (28). Eskridge reveals the result of their missionary reconnaissance:

> MacDonald began to contact various leaders in Bay Area evangelical circles that he felt were less hidebound by tradition and might be open to taking a chance on an unorthodox outreach in the Haight. Rather quickly, he drew together a mixed group of mostly Baptist pastors, laymen, and officials who were interested in the project. ... They dubbed their new nonprofit group Evangelical Concerns, Inc., printed some literature, and began to seek funds to establish a ministry center in the Haight that would provide some food for indigent hippies and support the Bay Area evangelicals' "missionary to the hippies, Ted Wise." (28)

Ted Wise and company started their outreach just in time.

5. The Living Room and the House of Acts

About 75,000 young people converged on San Francisco in 1967 (Eskridge 30), and they needed somewhere to stay and something to eat.

The Living Room mission in the Haight-Ashbury

By the end of that summer, Evangelical Concerns "had leased a storefront in the Armenian Hall on Page Street as a base to begin the evangelization of Haight-Ashbury." It was dubbed the Panhandle, the Mission, or as the press usually called it, the Living Room (29). Eskridge describes the place:

> The room itself was roughly twenty by forty and contained a large table, a white wicker couch, and a motley assemblage of chairs that could accommodate perhaps thirty wandering souls who might come in off the street at any one time. …
> From the limited funds available from Evangelical Concerns, occasional gifts from a few local churches and businessmen, and the gleanings of Wise and friends' wives… from local grocers' out-of-date foods, the Mission was able to feed its members and offer a cup of coffee, day-old doughnuts, or a bowl of hot soup to the neighborhood's wandering youth. (29)

Steve Heefner remembers their approach to the hippies that dropped in: "We were right up front; we'd say: 'Hey, we got soup here, we got soup and New Testament. You sit down and you eat the soup, you have to listen to the New Testament." Usually, it worked (31).

Although the coffee house lasted for only two years, they made contact with 30,000 to 50,000 young people (Enroth, Ericson Jr. and Peters 13).

The House of Acts in Novato

The Living Room wasn't the only outreach in the area. Eskridge explains that, after the Living Room/Mission got up and running in the Haight, the Wises, Doops, Heefners, and Sands finally found a suitable house—

> an old two-story, four-bedroom, two-bath farmhouse ("The House")—in the middle of a new subdivision in Novato.... Rented at $200 a month, the house had a big front porch, a large fenced yard, and a fireplace in the living room to add a bit of homey charm. (37)

A visiting member from First Baptist suggested they call the place the House of Acts, "because they were living like the first Christian community" (37).

Enter, Lonnie Frisbee

It was during this time that the guys from the downtown Mission encountered Lonnie on the streets, "waving a Bible and preaching about Jesus, flying saucers, and Christ consciousness" (33).

> Taking him in hand, they took him for some coffee to discuss his beliefs and eventually brought him to the group house, where he informed them that he had just had his own

personal theophany. ... Rescuing him from a bad living arrangement in the Haight, the group accepted Frisbee, and, after studying the Bible with the others, he eventually moved toward more orthodox views. (33)

This was the environment in which Lonnie was discipled. But Lonnie would never be known for his orthodoxy. Beginning to end, he was different.

6. Lonnie Begins Ministry

Following his conversion in the canyon, Lonnie immediately went to the beaches and preached about Jesus. People made fun of him, but he kept at it.

He would stand up in a public place and say, "Hey... *hey*! I've got something to tell you!" (Di Sabatino) And people would gather around him. He would share about Jesus, and people would give their lives to Christ. Soon Lonnie was baptizing these converts in the Pacific Ocean.

It seems the fruit was ripe for picking. Evangelist Ché Ahn says of the Jesus Movement: "[I]t was easy to lead people to the Lord. It was miraculous. People might approach you to ask what time it was, and you might say, 'It's time to get saved'— and they would!" (Ahn 98)

Lonnie moves in to the House of Acts

Ted Wise invited Lonnie to live with them at the commune in Novato. Lonnie found acceptance and a loving family life there. He called the ranch "the House of Acts," but it was commonly known as "the Big House" (Frisbee and Sachs 52–53, 56).

Shortly afterward, Lonnie withdrew from art school against the advice of its principal (56). He wanted to preach the gospel.

Lonnie ministers at the Living Room

Lonnie also hung out with Wise at the Living Room, which was open to anyone who wanted to drop in, hang out, eat soup, and talk God.

According to Coker, "Frisbee's roommates say no matter how many seekers came through their door, they'd all eventually wind up huddled around Lonnie" (Coker, First Jesus Freak).

Fellow Jesus freak Kent Philpott, a few years older than Lonnie, remembers that Lonnie "loved to talk theology and the Bible." Ted Wise and the others were more philosophically oriented, but Philpott says, "I could understand Lonnie and he understood me" (Philpott 62).

> His soft, easy manner drew people. He was not a dynamic or loud preacher; he was serious yet conversational. He identified with those who had lived a hard life and were searching for answers.

> Lonnie loved to roam the streets of the Haight and witness to the hippies about Jesus. On many occasions, I watched him begin a simple conversation with one hippie, which then turned into a preaching event, as people stopped and listened in. On some occasions, the crowd of hippies who gathered around Lonnie resulted in cars stopping and blocking streets. It was plain there was something about him—perhaps an anointing, a gift of evangelism, certainly a passion—but whatever it was, many were coming to Christ through his witness and testimony. (62–63)

At the Mission, they ministered to young people who were strung out on drugs, including girls who had run away and were headed towards prostitution. Lonnie claims that Charles

Manson showed up one day for soup (Frisbee and Sachs 57, 59, 61). Jim Doop remembered that Manson proclaimed he was God. Ted Wise laughed at him and said, "If you're God, I'm truly disappointed" (Eskridge 31).

Lonnie rejects the gay scene

The Big House and the Living Room were where Lonnie was discipled, eventually leaving behind his beliefs about Rainbow and UFOs. He was exposed to a lot in the city that summer; the district was a cauldron of different beliefs and lifestyles.

Lonnie mentions in *Not By Might Nor By Power* that the gay men he saw in the Haight "were way over the top."

> They strutted down the street with one another wearing hot pants and high heels. I said to myself, "Nah, I'm not going in that direction." … [T]he gay movement scared me. At that particular time in the Haight-Ashbury they *were* really like freaks grinding on one another as they marched past society. (Frisbee and Sachs 55)

Although Lonnie had participated in the gay scene in Laguna Beach and earlier in San Francisco, he expressed discomfort with its more flamboyant aspects. He was learning a different morality.

Because of the molestation he endured during adolescence, Lonnie, as did others at that time, connected homosexuality with pedophilia, although they are not related (Kort).[4] He called it "a dark, deceptive world" (Frisbee and Sachs 55).

---

4   "The empirical research does not show that gay or bisexual men are any more likely than heterosexual men to molest children" (Herek).

Lonnie Frisbee, soul-winner

To bring the light, Lonnie was always out winning souls. According to Enroth, Ericson, and Peters, "Soul-winning [was] his chief vocation" (93). He connected with an older couple, "hard core Pentecostals," who were street-preaching to the hippies.

Lonnie approached them and said, "I want to help you. I want you to teach me what to do, because I don't know what to do" (Frisbee and Sachs 63). So he connected with them, and they let him preach.

He drew a crowd and explained that, "Soon I was preaching the Gospel under the anointing of the Holy Spirit, and people were interested in what I had to say" (63–64).

Seeing the fruit of Lonnie's ministry, the man told Lonnie he was an evangelist. Lonnie didn't know what that meant.

The man told him, "That's somebody who leads people to Christ. We all need to share our faith, but there are also special callings. It's a gift in the ministry[5], and you have it" (64). He had it in spades.

At eighteen in the Haight-Ashbury, Lonnie began his spiritual career as an evangelist.

---

5   See Ephesians 4:11.

7. Speaking in Tongues in Southern California

Lonnie made a few month-long journeys back to southern California, where he open-air preached on the beaches, at Newport pier, and at free-speech areas on university campuses. "I could draw a crowd of people if I just opened my mouth," Lonnie admits (Frisbee and Sachs 66). This statement was confirmed by many who knew him.

He connected with a fledgling storefront ministry called Teen Challenge that ministered to drug addicts and street people (67). The leader, a guy named Bob, was the first person whom Lonnie heard praying in tongues—meaning, in his private prayer language (68).

Bob took him to a church where Lonnie could get filled with the Holy Spirit: Fullerton Foursquare (68). Foursquare is the denomination founded by dynamic Pentecostal evangelist Aimee Semple McPherson (1890–1944).

When the visiting evangelist at Fullerton Foursquare gave the altar call for the baptism in the Holy Spirit, Lonnie responded, recalling:

> [W]hen he laid his hands on my head—heaven came down!
> It wasn't a light fluffy experience. It was heavy oil—it was a
> heavy oil experience. The power of the Holy Spirit started
> coming down through him as an instrument of ministry, and

the power of God filled my whole body with about ten thousand volts of electricity.

I said in my mind, "How can I even survive this? How am I going to live through this experience?"

God filled every atom of my being with the resurrection power of Jesus Christ. There was not one ounce of my body that wasn't filled with the power of the Holy Spirit. (70)

This initiation made Lonnie bolder. "I led a lot of people to the Lord before I was baptized in the Holy Spirit, but after I was baptized, I was able to lead hundreds to Christ" (71).

Yet evangelism wasn't his only mission; by the end of 1967, Lonnie wanted to find a wife. He traveled south once more to find her.

8. Lonnie Takes a Bride

Connie Bremer came from a troubled family and had run away from home. She first met Lonnie "while selling him pot and LSD at a Silverado Canyon commune called the Brotherhood," pens Matt Coker in an interview with Connie (now Bremer-Murray).

"'He was kind of the clown to us,' she recalls about Lonnie. 'He was not groovy.' But she later witnessed this ungroovy clown's odd behavior lead to strange and wonderful things in the name of Jesus Christ" (Coker, Ears on Their Head).

Connie's conversion

Sometime later in Tahquitz Canyon, Lonnie encountered Connie again, sun-bathing in the nude. He writes:

> She had dropped some acid and was a run-away. I knew this girl and had witnessed to her before. She came from a very broken home. I gently started talking to her about the Lord. She was stoned, and I didn't want to blow her trip. I sat next to her, opened my Bible, and read to her. Soon there were tears flowing down her pretty cheeks. (Frisbee and Sachs 74)

The Spirit of God was able to cut through the haze of drugs to touch her heart. Connie testifies of her conversion experience:

I had known Lonnie from before when he used to come up to the canyon but didn't recognize him at first. All I remember was this guy walking up to me and reading out of the Bible. As he read his voice sort of faded out and God began to speak. "This is your opportunity now to accept Jesus Christ." I don't know why but I started to cry. I guess I realized that drugs were a bummer and there was no place else to turn. Through my tears I said I wanted to accept Christ. And I did! (Smith and Steven, Reproducers 40)

Lonnie baptized Connie in water there, perhaps in Green Tree Pool. He then took her north to the Novato ranch, where they lived for some time.

Having come from an abusive family situation, Connie recalls that the women at the House of Acts provided her first experience of stable family life. The period at the Big House was the first time she felt safe, saying, "I couldn't get enough of their love" (Eskridge 38).

Lonnie and Connie's relationship and marriage

During this time she and Lonnie should have been drawing closer. They did, but not in the way most young couples do. Instead, Connie says of Lonnie's courtship: "There was no hand-holding. I wasn't even interested in Lonnie in that way" (Di Sabatino). Lonnie gives no reason in his autobiography about why he wanted to marry Connie or marry anyone at all.

"He didn't get on his knees," Connie explains. "He didn't tell me he wanted to marry me because he loved me so dearly," she says with humor. "I don't know what I was thinking."

Sandi Heefner, one of the founding members of the Big House confesses, "I never could see those two together as a couple."

Because of rejection in her upbringing, Connie saw herself as undesirable. She admits she told Lonnie yes simply because he asked her (Di Sabatino).

"It wasn't very long after he asked me that I had misgivings about it," Connie says. She wrote Lonnie a letter explaining herself. It upset him, and he turned his back on her for a while. She called it "an emotional upheaval." Because she experienced his rejection—one of her trigger points—she acquiesced.

With flowers in their hair, they married in April 1968 (Di Sabatino).

9. Chuck Smith's Start in the Ministry

Charles Ward "Chuck" Smith (June 25, 1927 – October 3, 2013) attended junior college in Santa Ana and then graduated from L.I.F.E. Bible College (now LIFE Pacific College), a Pentecostal school affiliated with the International Church of the Foursquare Gospel, founded in 1923 by Aimee Semple McPherson (Life Pacific College).

The Smiths' early ministry

Chuck and his wife Kay entered denominational ministry with Foursquare in Prescott and Tucson, Arizona. Smith was also the campaign manager and worship director for healing evangelist and prophet Paul Cain in the early 1950s (Chuck Smith, pastor).

After enduring seventeen years in the ministry, Smith experienced a crisis. He confesses, "I came to the place where I could no longer digest the stifling restrictive role I was required to play. … There never seemed to be room for the Holy Spirit to work creatively among us" (Smith and Steven, Reproducers 14).

Bible studies lead to pastoring

Having purchased a home in Newport Beach, California, Chuck and Kay opened it up to small Bible studies. His desire to dispense with denominational "folderol" met with success, and the Bible groups expanded.

Along with the Newport Beach and other home groups, he had his own church in Costa Mesa. "By September of 1964 the home Bible studies became so large and demanding that Chuck resigned his Costa Mesa pastorate to give the home study program his full attention" (15). He felt he was meant to teach the Word.

The Corona, California, Bible study group invited him to hold Sunday services in the Corona American Legion Hall (16). This work also grew dramatically, and Chuck began teaching on radio station KREL. The Corona group invited him to stay and pastor. He moved the family but leased the house in Newport Beach.

However, soon after, Smith says he "began to feel a tug inside back to the beach area." The home study group still going in Costa Mesa invited him to return and promised financial support (17).

Smith joins floundering Calvary Chapel

A contractor told him about the problems they were having at his Costa Mesa church, Calvary Chapel, where the pastor wasn't interested in shepherding the work.

"We only have about twenty-five on Sunday morning and consider ourselves lucky if six to twelve come out on Sunday night. I know God has blessed you in Corona," the contractor told Smith, "but I wonder if you would consider moving to a new ministry."

"Yes," said Chuck with a smile. "I don't know why but, strange as it may seem, I would be interested. However, I don't know what my wife will say about this!" (17)

Two years previously, according to Bill Jackson, "God had sovereignly spoken to Chuck that he was going to become a shepherd over many flocks and that his ministry would grow so large that the building would not be able to hold the people" (Jackson, Quest 34).

Smith again moved his family—Kay and their children Jan, Chuck Jr., Jeff, and Cheryl—back to Newport Beach in December 1965, and he became assistant pastor of Calvary Chapel.

With all the moves, Kay questioned her husband's judgment. "After all," she said, "why would he want to leave our work in Corona, California? It was a growing congregation of over one hundred fifty. The people loved us. We had an important radio ministry, and Chuck left it all to be second man to a dwindling congregation of twenty-five" (Smith and Steven 13).

Yet within six months, Smith had implemented his plans to beautify the church, and membership doubled. It doubled again in the following six months. Smith had stumbled onto a formula for success: "People came to the home Bible studies," he explains, "got turned on and came to church for further instruction and fellowship" (Smith and Steven 25).

By the end of 1967 Smith and the Calvary board were considering property to build a larger church (25). They rented a Lutheran church building for a while. Later, the Greenville School fell into their hands, and there they began to build. Things were looking up for Smith and Calvary Chapel.

10. Lonnie Meets Pastor Chuck Smith

In *The Quest for the Radical Middle*, Bill Jackson informs, "Smith tried every gimmick possible to grow his church" (Jackson, Quest 33). But Smith encountered a turning point that changed everything. "After struggling seventeen years [in the ministry]," narrates Di Sabatino, "Lonnie Frisbee walked into his life" (Di Sabatino).

Smith considers hippies

The Big House in Novato was featured in the January 1968 issue of *Christian Life* magazine, with a mustachioed Ted Wise on the cover. Chuck Smith read the article, "God's Thing in Hippieville" (Eskridge 40), still wrestling with his feelings toward hippies. Then he met

> John Nicholson, a thin-faced young man with bright blue eyes, horn-rimmed glasses and neatly clipped long blond hair. ... John was more than just a young man the pastor's daughter [Jan] brought home from college. He was for many, including Chuck, their first close contact with the youth drug and hippie culture. John had lived and gone through the confusion and horror of Haight-Ashbury, but found the Lord through the witness of people from the San Francisco commune, House of Acts. (Smith and Steven 26)

Nicholson often went to the beach to witness, where it was routine for him to lead two or three young drug users to the Lord in an afternoon. "'I was talking to five kids who were stoned on acid,' he said to Chuck one day, 'and the Spirit used me to speak to them and all were converted'" (37). Smith asked the young man to bring him a hippie.

Nicholson was driving south to Orange County when he picked up a hitchhiker and began sharing his testimony with him.

> The hitchhiker let John speak for a few minutes then reached into his pocket and pulled out a Bible. "Far out, man," he said. "I'm a Christian too. I was just hitchhiking so I could witness to anyone who would pick me up."

> "Hey," John said, "that's great. Say, I wonder if you would like to meet some friends of mine. They've been wanting to meet a hippie for a long time. Man, when they see you with your beard and long hair and find out you're a Christian carrying a Bible, it'll blow their minds! By the way, my name's John. What's yours?"

> "Lonnie," he said. "Lonnie Frisbee." (37)

Nicholson introduces Lonnie to Chuck Smith

Nicholson brought Lonnie to the Smith home. Smith recalls that John had delivered to him "a real, honest-to-goodness hippie." About this meeting, he says: "Lonnie extended his hand, and there was such a warmth and love manifested in his greeting, I was caught off-guard. There was an instant bond.

There was a power of God's Spirit upon his life that was very easily recognized" (Frisbee Memorial Service).

Lonnie shares the significance of this first meeting from his side:

> I would venture to say that a divine appointment of heavenly significance manifested itself into the affairs of men. That might sound a little grandiose, but within a very short time, thousands and thousands of precious souls were added to the Kingdom of God, and a major move of the Spirit swept up the coast of California and around the world. It was a God-thing. (Frisbee and Sachs 78)

In *The Reproducers*, Chuck Smith and Hugh Steven recount the meeting this way:

> What the Smiths saw and felt almost did blow their minds! Not because they couldn't equate Christians with beards and long hair. But because they saw in this almost frail young man an unusual character and capacity to love. "This might be the very person to help us begin reaching the great numbers of hippies who are migrating to the beach areas," mused Chuck.
>
> As the evening progressed Chuck shared his dream with Lonnie and John. "If you could help John and a few of us share Christ with the hippies on the beach," said Chuck, "I believe they would respond. You speak their language and you know better than any of us how, what and why they think and feel the way they do. Furthermore you could stay with us for a couple of weeks and help me understand what makes them tick." (Smith and Steven 38)

Lonnie liked the idea but said he lived in San Francisco with his wife.

"No problem," Chuck said. "Bring her. She can stay too" (Smith and Steven 38). A few weeks later the Frisbees moved into the Smith home with a couple of other hippies.

Chuck Smith Jr said that his father invited Lonnie to speak at their Sunday evening service, which at that time ran thirty to forty people. "Lonnie made a hit. My parents begged him to come back" (Di Sabatino).

Lonnie learns not to mention homosexuality

Matt Coker claims, "During his first testimony at Calvary, Frisbee mentioned he'd rejected the homosexual lifestyle" (Coker, First Jesus Freak).

In an interview with Peter Chattaway of *Christianity Today*, David Di Sabatino adds, "His early testimony at Calvary Chapel was that he had come out of the homosexual lifestyle, but he felt like a leper because a lot of people turned away from him after that, so he took it out of his testimony" (Chattaway).

In fact, according to Kathy Baldock, Executive Director of Canyonwalker Connections, a ministry established to repair the breach between the conservative church and the LGBT Christian community, once Lonnie confessed his "sin" and he publicly rejected "the homosexual lifestyle," Lonnie was told to "never speak about it again in his testimonies" (Baldock, Walking the Bridgeless Canyon 352).

It's miraculous that God can save dirty hippies, but it overstretches the bounds of faith to say God can save gays. Di Sabatino comments, "I think that's an indictment of the church" (Chattaway).

Lonnie and Connie move to Orange County

Yet, in the early days, everything was hearts and flowers. Kay Smith said of the Frisbees, "We were fascinated with their genuine openness and reality. There was so much natural beauty and love bubbling forth we couldn't resist them," and "neither could the people at Calvary" (Smith and Steven 38–39).

After their visit with the Smiths, Lonnie and Connie returned to Novato. Connie loved living in the Big House. But Chuck Smith eventually called and invited Lonnie to join the staff at Calvary Chapel. Lonnie claims a fight ensued because Connie did not want to leave the ranch. He admits he pulled rank, and back to Orange County they went (Frisbee and Sachs 79).

11. Kay Smith's Prophecy

Kay Smith, Pastor Chuck Smith's wife, prophesied during the first Calvary Chapel service that Lonnie and Connie attended (Di Sabatino). According to her son Chuck Smith Jr, the message stated that Lonnie and Connie would have a worldwide impact to their ministry.

Lonnie recalls the prophecy, which came when fifteen people were seeking God at the altar:

> "Because of your praise and adoration before my throne tonight, I'm going to bless the whole coast of California." ... And when we started to receive the word *as* from God, the Spirit of the Lord fell upon us, and we began to weep. And the Lord began to give people visions of that prophecy. And the Lord continued on to say that it was going to move across the United States and then go to the different parts of the world. ... From that day on, we went to the beaches. (Lonnie Frisbee: Mother's Day)

Chuck Smith Jr said his parents believed that "all these people coming to Christ represented the new Church." In other words, **these dirty, counterculture hippies—despised and rejected by many believers at the time—were now the Body of Christ** (Di Sabatino).

It was a repeat in the psychedelic age of what happened in the early church when God poured out his Spirit on the Gentiles (see Acts 10:15, 19–20, 28–48; 11:1–18). This theme is about to repeat itself with those whom much of the church despises as an "abomination."

Lonnie began teaching on Wednesday evenings at Calvary Chapel, and the church packed out with hippies. Christian musician Chuck Girard says, "The doors blew open at that point, and Calvary grew from about 200 to 2000 in about a six-month period, and that was the beginning of what is now history" (Di Sabatino). "Lonnie Frisbee IS the story of Calvary Chapel" (Exclusive Interview).

12. The House of Miracles

The famous June 21, 1971, issue of *Time* featured the Jesus People Movement, proclaiming that "Communal 'Christian houses' are multiplying like loaves and fishes" (New Rebel Cry 56).

The Bluetop Motel and the House of Miracles

Seeking to reproduce the fruit of Novato's House of Acts and the San Francisco Living Room, Chuck Smith's church also procured a house and the Bluetop Motel. Lonnie says:

> When we first arrived in Costa Mesa, the Calvary Chapel congregation, which was about 80 people on a good Sunday, had rented a small house which Chuck named "the House of Miracles." He wanted to model it after our House of Acts up north. Several of us immediately converged on the beaches, and we led dozens and dozens of young people to the Lord right away. I would pray with them—and then bring them home. (Frisbee and Sachs 80)

Chuck Smith put Lonnie and Connie in charge of the two-bedroom House of Miracles with John and Jackie Higgins, young Catholics who had come into the born-again experience at Calvary. "It was May of 1968," says Jackson, "and time for an explosion" (Jackson, Quest 35). Within two weeks fifty young people were crowding into the house (Smith and Steven 43–44). The

Frisbees and the Higginses put the new converts to work evangelizing, and soon hundreds were being added to Calvary.

Susie Hendry, a young woman disenfranchised with her church and spiritual walk, ended up at the House of Miracles with a friend.

> We knocked at the door and a hippie long-haired type answered and invited us in. This was my first experience with this kind of person and I was kind of startled. He started talking about the Lord. He looked like a hippie but he was really right on! He told us about Calvary Chapel and invited us to come. We did and I've been going ever since. (12)

The Christian commune movement

The House of Miracles was the first of nineteen communal houses whose leaders later migrated to Oregon, where they formed Shiloh Youth Revival Centers, the largest and one of the longest lasting of the Jesus People communes. They expanded across North America to 175 communal houses with 100,000 members.

James Richardson suggests Shiloh may have been the largest Christian commune in U.S. history (Richardson). Bill Jackson states, "Other such communes would follow in a chain reaction, thus starting the Christian commune movement, one of the major vehicles reaching the drug culture" (Jackson, Quest 31).

Lonnie's connection to Benny Hinn

It was through a Shiloh branch in Oshowa, Ontario, Canada that healing evangelist Benny Hinn began his ministry in December 1974. Stan and Shirley Phillips arranged for him to speak at their church, Trinity Assembly of God.

Hinn says that despite a stuttering problem, the Holy Spirit anointed him to speak, and he concluded with a prayer, "Holy Spirit, you are welcome here. Please come." The power of God fell on the place, and people began dropping to the floor (Hinn 23, 25). This phenomenon also happened with Lonnie, another devotee of Kathryn Kuhlman, as we'll soon see.

From communes to church growth

Lonnie and others started Bible studies at the House of Miracles, took everyone to church, and then hit the beaches to evangelize.

"The church began to grow in leaps and bounds," recalls Lonnie, "with wall-to-wall, longhaired hippies, beards, beads and bare feet on Sunday mornings. It upset some of the old fogies in the congregation. However, most of them got over it when they saw the Lord moving so powerfully with us" (Frisbee and Sachs 80–81).

Either at the House of Miracles or the Bluetop Motel—Lonnie can't remember which—former high school classmate Jimmy Kempner came, causing a commotion on a bad LSD trip. Lonnie led him to the Lord, discipled him, and later Kempner preached to huge crowds at Knotts Berry Farm (82). Kempner was the first to preach at Disneyland, and was one of many whose ministries began through Lonnie's influence.

13. Pastor Greg Laurie Saved Under Lonnie's Ministry

It seemed Lonnie was everywhere, preaching and witnessing about Christ. He preached on the beaches. He ministered in church. He preached on college campuses and in high schools.

The Holy Spirit at Harbor High School

Lonnie recalls, "[W]e had Bible studies going in four major high schools—ON CAMPUS—which is now unheard of in 'liberated' America." The Bible study at Harbor High School had up to 150 kids in it, according to Lonnie, who ministered with Ray Rent of Bethesda Fellowship in Costa Mesa (Frisbee and Sachs 122). Lonnie reports:

> It was near the end of the school year. God had been visiting us in the science room. I will never forget the anointing that was on those meetings. ... It was off the scale. ... Sometimes the power of God would descend on everyone, and all the kids would fall on the ground under the power of the Holy Spirit. ... They would be speaking in tongues... the power of God struck everyone in the room, and we were *all* caught up in the Spirit, praying, seeing visions, and interceding for people to be saved. ... The bell would ring and the kids would still be lying under the power of the Holy Spirit all over the floor—everywhere! It was mind-blowing to see that kind of raw power fall on the students. (122–123)

Greg Laurie encounters Lonnie

It was here at Harbor High school that Lonnie preached to a group of students gathered on the lawn one hot day in 1971. Among them was a young man who came to faith and grew to be one of the most influential pastors and evangelists the U.S. has ever known: Greg Laurie.

Years ago, Laurie testified at Calvary Chapel about what happened that hot day.

> "During a lunch break in high school I decided to buy some acid. But before I got to buy it I ran into a group of kids singing songs. It sounded neat and I went over to find out what their thing was. Here were all these kids radiating a joy that I couldn't pinpoint. So I sat off to one side and listened. All they sang about was Jesus. Suddenly a little bearded guy gets up and tells us his name is Lonnie Frisbee and starts right in preaching from the Bible. It wasn't watered down or jazzed up to try and appeal to the kids. Just right out of the Word."
> (Smith and Steven 86)

In his 2008 biography *Lost Boy*, Laurie remembers it this way:

> Then one of the guys in the group stood up. He had a Bible in his hand, and shoulder-length dark hair and a beard. His brown eyes blazed. It was Lonnie Frisbee....
>
> He read a little bit from the New Testament, and then he talked about how Jesus wasn't just some far-off, far-out historical figure. How He was real. How He could be known personally.

I sat transfixed. This guy looked like a biblical character, and he related to me at that moment in my life. Then Lonnie said something that struck my heart: "Jesus said that 'You are either for Me, or you are against Me.' There's no middle ground with Jesus. You're either for Him or against Him... which side are you on?" (Laurie and Vaughn 88)

Greg strongly desired to receive this salvation that Lonnie said anyone could have by accepting Christ as personal Savior. When Lonnie extended the invitation, he wanted to go forward but stopped when he saw some of his old friends in the crowd. But something compelled him to move up front, where he prayed and accepted Christ.

"The second I started to pray I remember it felt like something was lifted off my back and all the sins I had ever committed were gone. I was free! It was just great! People came up and hugged me and told me how wonderful it was to know Jesus." (Smith and Steven 87)

Lonnie disciples Laurie

Lonnie reports Laurie was also baptized in the Holy Spirit at that outdoor meeting. "He became my little brother and spiritual son from that day forward," Lonnie says. "We were together almost every day.... He knew my schedule and followed me everywhere. He spent time with my family, and came to my meetings" (Frisbee and Sachs 126). Laurie recalls:

Because Lonnie was the resident celebrity, I was thrilled when he invited me over to his house one day to visit with him and his wife, Connie. It was like getting a backstage pass for a rock concert. I came into their funky little house, checking out all the usual hippie fixtures: macramé plant holders with philodendron vines trailing everywhere, stained-glass panes hanging in front of the windows, and Lonnie's detailed oil paintings of missions, such as San Juan Capistrano. (Laurie and Vaughn 106)

Laurie believes that "Lonnie was one of those characters in life whose whole was more than the sum of his parts. From far away he looked like a small, mild-mannered hippie. But up close, he had a powerful charisma of personality that was much bigger than his physical presence" (106).

Laurie enters ministry

Laurie was consumed with Christ. "I had a strange stirring within me," he says, "that maybe He had gifted me—of all people—to be an evangelist and a pastor. I couldn't imagine that I could follow in the footsteps of people I admired as much as Chuck Smith and Lonnie Frisbee. But, as I knew from my studies in the Bible, stranger things had happened" (107).

Laurie began pastoring at nineteen, taking over a youth Bible study Lonnie had started that met in an Episcopal church in Riverside. Lonnie's Bible study "had mushroomed to 300 kids," says Laurie, "and teenagers all over Riverside were coming to faith in Jesus" (114).

That Bible study grew: Greg Laurie is now head pastor of Harvest Christian Fellowship in Riverside, California, which has over 15,000 members (Harvest Christian Fellowship). This is just some of the spiritual fruit that God spawned through Lonnie during the Jesus People Movement.

14. Calvary Chapel Explodes

The Jesus Movement was far-reaching, and its epicenter seemed to be in southern California.

Greg Laurie explains that, during that time, "people were coming to faith in great numbers at Calvary Chapel, and the church was baptizing about 900 new believers every month at Pirates' Cove at Corona del Mar beach" (Laurie and Vaughn 101). Lonnie's Tahquitz Canyon vision of the sea of humanity was coming to pass.

Among many others, Chuck and Kay Smith took Greg Laurie under their wing and put him to work winning souls with Lonnie, about whom he says, "People from all over the area were coming to know Jesus because of Lonnie's ministry, just as I had. We followed him right into Calvary Chapel, and that's where we were grounded in our new faith. We came for Lonnie; we stayed for Chuck" (106).

Calvary Chapel's evolution

What was Calvary Chapel like at that time? A 1972 source tells us.

> At first glance the Chapel's red tile roof, arched portals and early California architecture resemble an affluent real estate office. ... The Chapel is located in an upper middle-class housing development on the borders of Costa Mesa and

49

Santa Ana. But this is no ordinary church building. (Smith and Steven 1)

It seated 1000, but another 500 gathered outside on the side portico—a far cry from the sparse attendance of years before. "When they ask about this [growth] I feel like a bystander," Smith said. "I remind them it's not Chuck Smith at work. It's God through His Holy Spirit turning people on" (9–10).

When the hippies turned up at the new church barefoot, some of the established members—"straight" in hippie lingo— had a problem.

> It was just that some of the members of Calvary were concerned with the balance of influence between the long- hairs and their own children. The regular members at Calvary were sincerely thankful to God for the success the communes were having. But when the young people came to church in larger numbers and sat on the floor during services, there were obvious tensions. (55)

However, once these members saw how genuine the young converts were, their hearts softened. Ex-Marine sergeant Glenn Jackson attests that, "The Lord, through Calvary, has helped us grow and become aware of our bigotry and narrow- ness" (56).

Some, though, asked Pastor Chuck to speak out against the hippies' dress code and their bad habit of flaking out on the lawn after church, reading their Bibles and smoking (57). With kindness and understanding, Smith responded to the older people:

"I don't want it ever said that we preach an easy kind of Christian experience at Calvary. But I also don't want to make the same mistake the Holiness church made thirty years ago. Without knowing it they drove out and lost a whole generation of young people with a negative no-movie, no-dance, no-smoke gospel. Let us at Calvary not be guilty of this same mistake. Instead let us trust God and emphasize the work of the Holy Spirit within individual lives. It's exciting and much more real and natural to allow the Spirit to dictate change. Let us never be guilty of forcing our western Christian subculture of clean shaven, short hair or dress on anyone. We want change to come from inside out." (57–58)

Such cultural changes were brought about by the invasion of hippies into an upper middle class church. It makes real the Jewish/Gentile controversy of the first-century church.

These struggles are not over. Will history repeat itself and love win out when today's church is faced with an influx of those unlike the majority? In more ways than one—for yesterday and today—Lonnie led the way in sparking global revival.

Lonnie sparked the growth

The KQED Arts department of *Truly CA* claims that "Lonnie Frisbee was the charismatic sparkplug that launched the 'little country church' into a worldwide ministry, and propelled some of its then fledgling leaders into some of the most powerful movers and shakers of the evangelical movement" (Frisbee: KQED).

Lonnie shares in his autobiography about the phenomenal growth of the early days when Calvary Chapel was just getting started.

In no time at all there were over a thousand people at each of our meetings. Chuck went to two services on Sunday morning and eventually to three. We started baptizing new believers in the ocean, and the baptisms themselves began to explode with the Spirit of God touching everyone. People were getting saved as they came to watch others get baptized, and then being baptized themselves right on the beach at Corona Del Mar minutes later. (Frisbee and Sachs 83)

Coker describes Chuck Smith and Lonnie standing "side by side off Little Corona beach, dunking thousands of young people in the chilly waters for the most informal and joyous of baptisms" (Coker, First Jesus Freak).

In *The History of Calvary Chapel*, Smith writes, "One estimate put the total number of Calvary Chapel (Costa Mesa) baptisms performed over a two-year period during the mid-1970s at well over 8,000. Additionally, over 20,000 conversions to the Christian faith took place during that same period" (Smith, History of Calvary Chapel 2).

Kathy Baldock reveals that between 1968 and 1971, "Frisbee brought several thousand new Christian converts to Calvary Chapel" (Baldock, Walking the Bridgeless Canyon 352).

"Church membership skyrocketed," says Coker. "Calvary and Vineyard have each propagated about 1,000 churches across the planet" (Coker, First Jesus Freak). "According to church growth experts, Calvary Chapel's 10-year growth rate was almost 10,000 percent!" (Smith, History of Calvary Chapel 2)

Besides the move of the Holy Spirit, what was the foundation for such explosive growth?

The Spirit and the Word

Lonnie praises Chuck Smith's Bible teaching, which grounded him in the Word of God and anchored his revelations from the Holy Spirit

Smith believed that the church's primary job is to bring glory to God. After this, its responsibility is not to evangelize, but instead to "build up believers for the work of ministry so they can reach maturity in Christ." If he equipped the church in this way, God showed him that Jesus would grow it (Smith, History of Calvary Chapel). In fact, as Bill Jackson points out, "the evangelism did not begin until Chuck stopped trying to be an evangelist and settled down to be a pastor-teacher, systematically teaching his church the Bible" (Jackson, Quest 38).

Lonnie says of "Papa Chuck": "He was instantly the hippie's father figure, and you know my history with father figures. I desperately needed a good and godly role model" (Frisbee and Sachs 84). So did many others.

Wednesday nights with Lonnie

Smith gave Lonnie every Wednesday night to minister. Lonnie desired to serve God and did his best to do so (85). He recalls:

> The Wednesday night meetings were glorious. [God's] presence and anointing [were] on every single meeting. Hundreds and then thousands came out to a mid-week church service in Orange County, California. ... Every seat was filled, the aisles were full, the front was packed with kids sitting on the floor, outside was packed with people listening on speakers, and looking in the windows. (86)

Lonnie would preach and then extend the invitation, and the altar would fill up with those wanting to accept Christ.

Jackson claims, "During the Jesus Movement, Lonnie had been one of the most powerful evangelists, instrumental in the explosion of Calvary Chapel through his preaching on Wednesday nights" (Jackson, Quest 71). Di Sabatino says that people noted Lonnie's "tremendous personal magnetism and his ability to relate the Christian message in the relaxed vernacular of the times" (382). Brian Vachon dubs him an "irresistible evangelist" (Vachon 91).

> His four years while employed at Calvary Chapel in Costa Mesa, California, serving as an evangelistic liaison between the church and the hippie counterculture from 1968 to 1971, radically transformed that church from a small two hundred member congregation to a thriving internationally renowned ministry (Jackson, Quest 378).

The ministry at the church and the baptisms in Pirate's Cove caught the attention of the media. When Lonnie was twenty-one, he says *Time* magazine, the BBC, and local KQED were all at one Wednesday night meeting. *Time* published its cover story, "The New Rebel Cry: Jesus is Coming!" on June 21, 1971 (Frisbee and Sachs 89).

However, this wasn't the highlight of those Wednesday evenings for Lonnie. During one fateful meeting, Lonnie's mother showed up. He didn't know she was there, but he felt impressed to extend the altar call for one more hesitant person.

His mother later told him, "As you were saying that somebody had to come forward, I looked up, and you turned into a white light! All I could see on the platform where you were standing was a ball of white light with three rainbows coming out of it!" (91)

Impelled to come forward, she accepted Christ on the spot.

15. Lonnie and Kathryn Kuhlman

Kathryn Kuhlman (1907–1976) was an American evangelist and faith healer mightily anointed by the Holy Spirit. From the 1940s into the 70s she traveled around the U.S. and the world holding healing crusades.

Kuhlman had a weekly national TV program in the 60s and 70s called *I Believe in Miracles*. In her later years she supported the fledgling Jesus People Movement (Kathryn Kuhlman).

Lonnie follows Kuhlman

For seven years Lonnie attended Kuhlman's monthly meetings at the Los Angeles Shrine Auditorium where he witnessed many miracles of healing. "The presence of the Holy Spirit would be so powerful," he said, "that it was overwhelming." Like Benny Hinn, another follower of Kuhlman's, Lonnie longed for the gifts of healings and miracles in his own life and ministry (Frisbee and Sachs 94). He confesses,

> Little did I know that God would answer my heart's desire, and there would come a day when I would be ministering alongside Kathryn Kuhlman at places like the Hollywood Palladium. There would also come a day when I would witness blind eyes opened beneath my hands. This unusual and unique woman taught me about the Holy Spirit, and she is my absolute hero in the faith. (95)

Lonnie credits Chuck Smith for teaching him the Bible and Kathryn Kuhlman for training him in the Holy Spirit. Lonnie's autobiography, written with the help of Roger Sachs, *Not By Might Nor By Power: The Jesus Revolution*, is dedicated to Kathryn Kuhlman (123).

In 1971 Kuhlman extended an invitation to Chuck Smith and Duane Pederson, founding editor of the *Hollywood Free Paper*. Pederson has often been credited with coining the terms "Jesus people" and "Jesus Movement" (Duane Pederson). Smith and Pederson took several busloads of young people to Kuhlman's studio in Hollywood to be featured and interviewed on her television show. From *The Jesus People*:

> The shaky alliance of the youthful revolutionaries with classical Pentecostalists is typified by long-time evangelist Kathryn Kuhlman. In a series of telecasts made in late summer '71, the Kuhlman ministry awkwardly but publicly joined hands with the saints of the movement. Standing among Chuck Smith ("Daddy Chuck," she called him), Lonnie Frisbee, and Duane Pederson, "Mama Kathryn" displayed an unconcealed eagerness to identify with the movement.... (Enroth, Ericson Jr. and Peters 151)

Although Lonnie had attended many of Kuhlman's meetings, these video recordings captured their first face-to-face encounter. David Di Sabatino's documentary, *Frisbee: The Life and Death of a Hippie Preacher*, contains footage from one of these shows in which Lonnie speaks (Di Sabatino). Clips are also available on YouTube.[6]

Kuhlman lays hands on Lonnie for impartation

Before Kuhlman died in 1976, she laid hands on Lonnie and prayed a prayer of impartation. But she's not the only woman who influenced Lonnie and his ministry. Lonnie shares,

> I believe that the anointing that is resting on my life can be traced directly to another woman of God—Aimee Semple McPherson, because of her influence to both Kathryn Kuhlman and Chuck Smith. Chuck came out of the Foursquare Church founded by Aimee, and Aimee... definitely influenced Kathryn Kuhlman. (Frisbee and Sachs 97)

When Kuhlman interviewed him on her show, Lonnie testified that Christ had changed his heart. With some disappointment, he later shares, "My critics will jump on this confession of faith that I made at 22 years of age, because of my future failures" (104).

Yet, "If anything comes out of my story," Lonnie writes, "it has to be a revelation that Jesus is real. That is my heart's desire and passion! That you and everyone would discover him. Jesus *is* alive!" (105)

---

6   YouTube: https://www.youtube.com/watch?v=gCvH9NOTSzw
https://www.youtube.com/watch?v=dJU-qA34p1w
https://www.youtube.com/watch?v=iAUysE3VE58.

16. Frisbees' Marriage on the Rocks

Despite what God was doing by his Spirit in those early years of the revival, not everything was perfect. For the first four years of his walk with Jesus, Di Sabatino narrates, "Lonnie spent every waking moment in ministry activity at Calvary Chapel. This schedule strained the Frisbees' marriage" (Di Sabatino).

Smith says ministry more important than marriage

Connie asked her pastor, Chuck Smith, for marital counseling, during which she spoke about her husband's overwork and unavailability.

Smith told her, "The most important thing is that souls are being saved."

Chuck Smith Jr believes his father's philosophy of ministry "harmed Lonnie and Connie's marriage." Connie herself felt she was "fighting God" for her husband's attention (Di Sabatino).

Smith and Lonnie at odds

Smith and Lonnie did not see eye to eye about ministry.

Chuck Smith Jr reveals that, although they had Pentecostal theology, his parents were uncomfortable with some of the practices and physical manifestations that came with the Holy Spirit revival in the Jesus People Movement.

Jackson explains that Smith minimized the use of the more charismatic gifts. "Tongues and prophecy are not allowed to manifest in the main services; other venues are provided for their expression. He does not want the services to be a 'circus'" (Jackson, Quest 38). Christian musician Debbie Kerner-Rettino claims that Smith told Lonnie, "If you pray for people and they fall down, you're going to lose your job" (Di Sabatino).

Lonnie's ministry marginalized

Lonnie's demonstrative ministry was shunted into more private believers' meetings called "Afterglows" (Di Sabatino). Authors of *The Jesus People* remark that

> Frisbee seems more preoccupied than the other pastors with charismatic manifestations, and one gets the distinct impression that he is more or less "kept in line" by the older staff members. ... If he determines that the person he is talking to is already a believer, his main concern is to have him experience the Baptism of the Spirit and speak in tongues. (Enroth, Ericson Jr. and Peters 93)

"Smith," says Di Sabatino, "made it clear to Frisbee that these times of Pentecostal experimentation could only take place subsequent to the preaching and teaching of the Bible" (Jackson, Quest 384).

Lonnie leaves Calvary

As a result of this curtailment, Lonnie decided to leave Calvary Chapel.

Smith discounted Pentecostalism, maintaining that love was the greatest manifestation of the Holy Spirit while Frisbee was strongly involved in theology centering on spiritual gifts and New Testament occurrences. Frisbee announced that he would leave California altogether and go to a movement in Florida led by Derek Prince and Bob Mumford which taught a pyramid shepherding style of leadership and was later coined as the Shepherding Movement. (Lonnie Frisbee: Wikipedia)

Lonnie and Connie left Calvary Chapel in 1971 because Lonnie felt his Pentecostal gifts were not appreciated and that "Chuck Smith's restrictions were too stringent." Chuck Smith Jr mentions they felt Lonnie's leaving was "a great betrayal" (Di Sabatino).

Whether or not the following comment is about Calvary remains unknown, but Lonnie said that he'd "been hurt real bad" in the ministry:

> I hate to say it, but in the height of the revival my wife and I were on food stamps! The church paid me twenty-five dollars a week, which for a married couple made us eligible for public assistance. It produced a growing resentment and wound in my life. In addition my wife felt isolated and left out as my responsibilities kept me going in a million directions. It caused *so* much strife between us. (Frisbee and Sachs 135)

17. Shepherding in Southern Florida

The Frisbees moved to Fort Lauderdale, Florida, in 1971 to work on their marriage under Bob Mumford, one of several ministers responsible for what is known as the Shepherding Movement or Discipleship Movement.

> It began when four well-known Charismatic teachers, Bob Mumford, Derek Prince, Charles Simpson, and Don Basham, responded to what they saw as a moral failure in a charismatic ministry in South Florida. Witnessing this failure, the four men felt mutually vulnerable without greater accountability structures in their lives. They also felt the charismatic movement was becoming individualistic and subjective. These realizations led them to mutually submit their lives and ministries to one another. Ern Baxter was later added to the core leadership of the group, and they became known as the "Fort Lauderdale Five." (Sheperding Movement: Wikipedia)

Lonnie had been introduced to Mumford as his Bible teacher at Melodyland School of Theology in Anaheim, California.

The Holy Spirit Teaching Mission

In *The Shepherding Movement*, David Moore explains that Mumford moved to Fort Lauderdale in August 1970 at the invitation of Eldon Purvis, who had started a Bible study that grew into the Holy Spirit Teaching Mission. The HSTM had launched *New Wine* magazine in 1969 with contributing writers Don Basham, Derek Prince, Charles Simpson, and Bob Mumford (Moore 25–27).

"In the summer of 1971," says Moore, "Bob Mumford invited several young men, most of whom were in successful youth ministries in the Jesus Movement, to move to Ft Lauderdale to be discipled by him as a kind of discipleship experiment" (50).

When Lonnie received Mumford's letter, he quit his position as youth pastor at Calvary and with Connie followed Mumford to Florida. "I had a desperate need for a father figure," admits Lonnie, "and a desperate desire to save my marriage" (Frisbee and Sachs 137).

The young men met with Mumford early each morning for prayer, worship, and training (Moore 50). Enroth indicates Lonnie joined the group "for a period of intensive Bible study" (Enroth, Ericson Jr. and Peters 93).

Smith denounces Derek Prince

Lonnie states that, some months before the move, Chuck Smith in an elders meeting denounced Derek Prince as a false prophet, a "wolf in the midst," claiming that Prince put too much emphasis on demonic deliverance (Frisbee and Sachs 138)—something Lonnie himself still practiced behind closed doors at Calvary against Smith's wishes (117).

At first wary of the man, Lonnie overcame his bias and grew to admire Prince, saying his mentor was "one of the most revered, honest, biblically balanced, and gloriously anointed apostles I have ever met in the Body of Christ." Prince ended up becoming the Frisbees' landlord in Fort Lauderdale (140–141).

Lonnie's missionary work with Mumford

During this time, Lonnie attended the newly planted Bible school and participated in several foreign mission trips led by Mumford and others to places such as Sweden, Poland, Germany, Israel, and Africa (143, 145). Lonnie reveals that,

> The Lord kept my missionary passion burning strong during this period of my life. It was foundational for the deeper call of the Great Commission that God was leading me into. ... I am intrigued by different cultures, and the Spirit of God captured my heart with a huge burden for homeless, abandoned children around the world in poverty stricken nations. I also love to travel. God put it all in my DNA. (143)

Mumford provides marital counseling

Connie shares in Di Sabatino's documentary that she went to Bob Mumford and told him what had been happening with her and Lonnie's marriage. She recounts,

> "He brought Lonnie in with me, and we sat down and talked, and he said [to Lonnie], 'Brother, you have got to be on track with your wife. You have got to be one person here. You can't have both of you going in two different directions, because your whole marriage is going to crumble. And if your marriage crumbles, your whole ministry is going to crumble. Everything's just going to go down the tubes.'" (Di Sabatino)

These words turned out to be prophetic.

Mumford asked Lonnie to step out of ministry for a year, get a regular job, support his wife, and knit a relationship. Lonnie did lay down his public ministry and took a construction job, he says, "hauling cement like my stepfather had done most of his non-military life" (Frisbee and Sachs 143).

Connie believes Lonnie said yes on the outside but no on the inside. She frankly admits, "I don't think that Lonnie really ever should have been married to anybody" (Di Sabatino).

Shepherding Movement goes sour

Although the Shepherding Movement may have started with good intentions, it ended up being seen by many as a hierarchical chain of control that became—not just for Lonnie, but for thousands of believers—a form of bondage.

Lonnie confessed later in a 1982 retreat, "One of the biggest mistakes that I have ever made in my walk in God was that I turned over my free will to another individual. *Don't ever do it.* If you have, take it back, because it's really a big sin against God" (Di Sabatino).

Yet Connie maintains that Mumford wasn't the enemy. She says, "Bob Mumford was the only rationally sane person that I had ever met because he saw the huge need to disciple people. And just because the discipleship thing turned into some kind of movement that got twisted doesn't mean that that truth wasn't truth" (Di Sabatino).

Lonnie concludes their time in Fort Lauderdale with these words:

By the Grace of God he was with us during our entire time in Florida, even though the heavy-handed effects of the

Shepherding Movement were taking their toll on our lives and on our marriage. It was absolutely one of the most difficult periods of my life. (Frisbee and Sachs 145)

Leaving this trying experience behind, Lonnie and Connie drove back west to southern California.

18. The Marriage Crumbles

Although Lonnie did step out of ministry for a year and he and Connie attempted to work on their relationship in Florida, their marriage ultimately failed.

Lonnie's story

Connie allegedly got involved in an affair with a man in the church they were attending. In his autobiography, Lonnie tells his side of the story:

> [M]y marriage was destroyed with an adulterous affair while I was in the peak of this ministry success. My wife was living in open adultery, in full view of the flock of God that we had raised up. She decided to have an affair with another born again Christian. … She lived with this man, a former friend of mine, in my house for one year, and the hate built up. She was still married to me. (Frisbee and Sachs 192)

Lonnie recalls that late one night he received a knock on the door. It was Connie's lover, who is never named.

"He had discovered her making love to his best friend," Lonnie says. "He broke down weeping in my arms" (192–193).

They talked all night about Jesus. The following morning, he asked Lonnie to baptize him, so they went down to the San Lorenzo River in Santa Cruz. There, they both received forgiveness and healing (193).

But Lonnie's isn't the only side of the story.

Connie's story

Connie reveals that "At the end of the marriage, [Lonnie] told me he had been staying late in some gay bars" (Di Sabatino). This apparently had been going on for some time.

Despite all their efforts, their shortcomings ended in breakup. They divorced in 1973.

Lonnie and Connie part ways

Connie says that after the divorce,

> I wanted to go where nobody knew my name. I didn't want to cause God any grief. I'd gotten caught up in an adulterous affair. I moved up to Meadow Vista in Placer County. I kind of went my own way. It's not that I stopped thinking about God—I was mad at him. He wasn't doing what I wanted him to do. (Coker, Ears on Their Head)

She ran into Lonnie while delivering UPS packages in Nevada City three years after they parted. "From that point on," Connie says, "Lonnie and I stayed in touch on the phone, or he'd come up and visit me, or I'd come down and visit him" (Coker, Ears on Their Head). Connie later re-married.

Recalling the struggle of their ministry years, Connie shares this:

> You worry about meals. I'd see all these people eating when Calvary's coffers were full. And we were poor. Chuck Smith never paid Lonnie. One day, Lonnie came home and said, "You'll never believe it: they hired somebody full-time to help Pastor Chuck." That blew him away.

Chuck and Kay Smith never came by to ask if I needed food. I went to the same grocery store she did; it's just that she went through the front door, and I went to the Dumpster in the back so that I could feed people. There was a disparity between what people believed to be happening and what was happening. I think Lonnie paid a huge price for that disparity. (Coker, Ears on Their Head)

Lonnie concludes the era of their relationship with these words from his biography:

It was not all Connie's fault. I need to say that. I know that I definitely am not the easiest person to live with. In the final analysis—I lost my marriage in the ministry. It is something that is not supposed to happen. (Frisbee and Sachs 195)

19. Lonnie Returns to Calvary Chapel

According to Di Sabatino, following the Frisbees' divorce, Lonnie moved north to Santa Cruz where he got involved with the Mission Street Fellowship. Then, "after five years of fumbling through a series of odd jobs and missionary jaunts, Lonnie decided to reconcile his relationship with Chuck Smith" (Jackson, Quest 385).

Lonnie called Smith and asked to return to Calvary Chapel, Costa Mesa. Lonnie was struck with the intervening success of the movement during his time away.

> What a blessing. What a miracle! It was my second tour of duty with Calvary Chapel. Calvary had grown to immense size with multiplied thousands of people, a huge new facility, a fully accredited school, and hundreds of new churches being planted or adopted under their umbrellas. I lost count of the Calvary Chapels around the world. (Frisbee and Sachs 191–192)

Di Sabatino confirms that, in four years, Calvary Chapel had become a movement with satellite churches all over the southwestern U.S. and thousands of members.

Lonnie was hired back as an assistant pastor but, says Di Sabatino, "Smith made it clear that the spiritual experimentation previously afforded him would no longer be tolerated" (Jackson, Quest 395).

Lonnie ministered in Afterglows, believers' meetings that shielded the greater congregation from demonstrative manifestations of the Holy Spirit. He also traveled as an evangelist with Calvary Chapel and Maranatha! Music (Frisbee and Sachs 195).

Unfortunately, their renewed relationship did not work out (Baldock, Walking the Bridgeless Canyon 354). Lonnie's homosexuality had not gone away, and it "eventually ruptured his friendship with Chuck Smith" (Turner).

Lonnie moved on to connect with another key church planter who came out of the Jesus Movement.

20. Lonnie Meets John Wimber

John Richard Wimber (February 25, 1934 – November 17, 1997) was a musician, pastor, and "one of the founding leaders of the Vineyard Movement, a neocharismatic Evangelical Christian denomination which began in the USA and has now spread to many countries world-wide" (John Wimber).

Wimber's early life and conversion

He was born in Kirksville, Missouri. Jackson reveals that Wimber's "father abandoned him on the day he was born and he was raised as an only child. He grew up learning nothing about God" (Jackson, Quest 43).

Wimber was musically inclined and learned to play several instruments. He played keyboard for the band *The Paramours*. In 1962 he bought *The Righteous Brothers*, playing saxophone for them (43–44). He became successful in the music business. "Music was to John what the ocean is to a fish. ... Between 1950 and 1962 he gained ninety percent of his income from teaching, directing, orchestrating and recording music" (44).

Although Wimber's family wasn't religious, he became a Christian in 1963. At a home Bible study led by Quaker Gunner Payne (White 162), Wimber's wife Carol dropped to her knees, weeping and repenting of her sins. At first puzzled, Wimber explains, "I ended up on the floor, sobbing, nose running, eyes watering, every square inch of my flesh perspiring profusely." All he could do was cry out, "Oh, God!" (Jackson, Quest 47)

Wimber evangelizes Yorba Linda, starts church

After this the Wimbers attended a Quaker church in Yorba Linda, California, and he led hundreds into Christian faith. By 1970 he was leading eleven different Bible study groups with more than 500 people (History of Vineyard).

> In 1974 he became the Founding Director of the Department of Church Growth at the Charles E. Fuller Institute of Evangelism and Church Growth, which was founded by the Fuller Theological Seminary and the Fuller Evangelistic Association. He directed the department until 1978. In this time a House Church began to form in his home. This group began to embrace some of the beliefs of the Charismatic Movement. This resulted in a split with the Quaker church that this group belonged to. (John Wimber)

This fledgling church outgrew the Wimber home and became the Anaheim Vineyard Christian Fellowship in 1977. But it was first associated with Calvary Chapel.

> After initially joining Calvary Chapel, the church had some differences with the Calvary Chapel leadership, relating mainly to the practice of spiritual gifts, [Wimber's] rejection of traditional Dispensationalism, and his embrace of Kingdom theology. As a result, they left Calvary Chapel to join a small group of churches started by Kenn Gulliksen, known as Vineyard Christian Fellowships, which became an international Vineyard Movement. (John Wimber)

Lonnie meets Wimber

Di Sabatino says that since Chuck Smith had dropped the hard-line Pentecostal stance and focused on comprehensive Bible teaching, Lonnie again realized he wasn't a good fit. He longed for an outlet for his more demonstrative Pentecostal style of ministry (Di Sabatino).

He connected with Wimber at a pastors' conference. Wimber's wife, Carol, tells the story.

> Lonnie Frisbee, who Chuck had apparently taken under his wing again, after Lonnie's foray into the Shepherding movement, came over to John and me and, without a word or an introduction, grabbed my head between his hands and asked John, "May I pray for your wife?" He was rather wild-looking, but I had heard the stories and knew who he was. This creature with all the hair, whose hands were planted in my hair, was one of the main players of the Jesus People Movement!

> "Sure, help yourself. Pray for her!" John agreed. It's funny now, neither of them thought to ask me, although I was honoured to have Lonnie pray on my head. He prayed that I would know the wolf when he came to our door, that God would alert me when John was in danger. It was strange, but then no stranger than everything else, and quite wonderful.

> In retrospect, if his prayer "took" so to speak, I wonder why Lonnie didn't alarm me, himself. Poor tormented Lonnie. **Running, trying to hide from his shame, but always landing in the middle of a move of God, unable to escape his calling. The gifts and the call of God are without repentance, the Bible tells us.** (C. Wimber 146, emphasis mine)

Carol paints Lonnie as a wild character, albeit one she respects. She also views him as a tragic figure, haunted by shame, yet unable to escape his calling and the anointing God had destined him for.

Carol says Lonnie told her and John that Chuck Smith had given him permission to come to the Wimbers' church. He showed up and hung around them occasionally over the next few years (146).

God told Wimber that he would join with Lonnie, but it took three years to happen because of Lonnie's reluctance (Lonnie Frisbee: Mother's Day). Yet there was much preparation going on in the background.

> Wimber had witnessed the explosive growth of Calvary Chapel and sought to build a church that embraced the healings and miracles that he had previously been taught were no longer a part of Christian life. He began teaching and preaching about spiritual gifts and healings which did occur, but it wasn't until May 1980 when Frisbee testified that the charismatic gifts of the Holy Spirit took hold of the church (Lonnie Frisbee: Wikipedia).

During the 1970s, Wimber realized that "the key to effectiveness was a combination of *proclamation* and *demonstration* of the gospel" (Jackson, Quest 53). Carol said, "Instead of show and tell, this is tell and show" (70).

Lonnie comes to dinner

The Wimbers invited Lonnie for dinner. Lonnie brought his roommate John Ruttkay, and around the table "they fellowshipped together about all the things that God had done" (71).

They decided that Lonnie would come to minister at Calvary Chapel, Yorba Linda. Carol Wimber explains:

> Now Lonnie Frisbee made [John] nervous; he made us all nervous, but John thought the Lord was telling him to ask Lonnie to speak, to give his testimony on the following Sunday night, which just happened to be our third anniversary as a church. It was 11 May 1980, Mothers' Day. (C. Wimber 146–147)

Jackson confirms, saying, "John at first balked at the idea because Lonnie's ministry style had a reputation for being controversial." But God had spoken to Wimber to have Lonnie speak at his church (Jackson, Quest 71).

Di Sabatino says that "Wimber had wanted to know why the miracles that happened in the Bible weren't happening today. He was about to learn why" (Di Sabatino).

21. The Holy Spirit Falls: Mother's Day 1980

As had happened at Calvary, Lonnie's ministry ushered the power of the Holy Spirit into what would become the Vineyard Movement. It began at Calvary Chapel, Yorba Linda, which in two years under Wimber's ministry had grown to about 700 members (Jackson, Quest 71).

John Wimber invites Lonnie to speak

In *Power Evangelism*, published in 1986, Wimber begins the account in this manner, mentioning Lonnie not by name, but only as "young man":

> It was Mother's Day, 1979[7], and I had invited **a young man** to speak at the evening service of the church of which I had only recently become pastor, what would later become the Vineyard Christian Fellowship in Anaheim, California. His background was the California "Jesus People" movement of the late sixties and early seventies and, so I heard, he was unpredictable when he spoke. I was apprehensive about him, but I sensed God wanted him to speak nevertheless. He had been used by God to lead Christians into a refreshing experience of the Holy Spirit, and it was obvious to me that the congregation needed spiritual renewal. I hasten to point out

---

7   Many other sources, including Carol Wimber and Bill Jackson, say 1980.

that asking this young man to speak went contrary to my normal instincts as a pastor. I take seriously the admonition that pastors are to protect their flocks, but in this instance I sensed it was what God wanted. Regardless, I was to stand by the decision, whatever the cost.

When he eagerly agreed to speak, I became even more apprehensive. What will he say? What will he do to my church? The Lord gently reminded me, "Whose church is this?" (Wimber and Springer 24, emphasis mine)

Lonnie's message

Carol Wimber recalls that her husband opened the service and introduced Lonnie, but remained on the platform behind his keyboard the whole time Lonnie spoke. "Within reach, should anything goofy occur" (C. Wimber 147). John invited Lonnie to share as the Lord led him.

Lonnie greeted the congregation gathered in the gymnasium (White 158) of Canyon High School (Jackson, Quest 63) with: "It's a joy to be here tonight and represent Jesus Christ." He soon told them that Wimber's church was his new home. "John and I have decided that we're going to move together in the Lord. And he's going to help me when I'm down, and you're going to be my family in Jesus. I feel welcome here."

The congregation responded with applause.

"I think the Lord's going to meet us tonight in a special way," Lonnie told them, "so **I want you to be in expectancy for a move of the Spirit of God**" (Lonnie Frisbee: Mother's Day).

Lonnie shared his background, beginning with the Haight-Ashbury era. He referred to himself as a "nudist vegetarian hippie" and made many humorous remarks about himself during his testimony.

Then he said, "I sense that we're experiencing a second wave of God. **I believe that we're having an outpouring of the Holy Spirit, something similar to what I sensed back then, eleven years ago.** I sense it in the atmosphere. I sense it in the eyes, I sense it in the voices of the people that I hear responding to the Lord in this hour. God is moving upon you in a very blessed way, and some of you are just new to it, you're just being introduced to it, and I always thought it would continue on and on, and it was always going to be the same. But, you know, revival doesn't always continue on. And I want to encourage you tonight to go on in what God is doing—press *in* to it" (Lonnie Frisbee: Mother's Day).

Wimber picks up the story, saying, "That evening he gave his testimony, a powerful story of God's grace. As he spoke, I relaxed. Nothing strange here, I thought" (Wimber and Springer 24). Wimber apparently spoke too soon.

Since his early days at Calvary Chapel, Costa Mesa, Lonnie's emphasis had shifted from evangelism to more demonstrative manifestations of Holy Spirit power, and Wimber and company were unprepared for what was about to happen.

Lonnie explained that he had returned to the Calvary Chapel staff after "getting involved in some spiritual error that the enemy almost wiped me out with," referring to the Shepherding Movement. He admitted, "I was cast down but not forsaken. Chuck was gracious, very gracious to me, to give me another opportunity to come back and minister at Calvary." He spoke about his missionary journeys by faith (Lonnie Frisbee: Mother's Day).

Then Lonnie recounted the story of Calvary's great growth, crediting the wisdom of the older believers and the zeal of the youth. He told the Vineyard congregation they were a model of what God wanted to do in the Church.

"Learn, move, flow," he admonished them. **"The Lord tonight is saying to you, 'Come, let's go into a greater dimension.'"**

He preached on Isaiah 60:1–5: "Arise, shine, for your light has come, and the glory of the Lord rises upon you." He said, **"We're going to see the Lord in our midst. He's moving down the aisles"** (Lonnie Frisbee: Mother's Day).

John White describes Wimber's initial reaction to Lonnie's message: "He was relieved when the young man gave a sound and straightforward address, introducing no heterodox views to the congregation" (White 158).

Yet Carol Wimber remembers that notable service and Lonnie's ministry with these words:

[Lonnie] was articulate and profound and funny, and John's fears were put to rest as he enjoyed Lonnie along with everyone else. That is, until the end. After the hilarious applause, John, full of good cheer, made a move to get up from the keyboard to take the mike and close the meeting. He wasn't fast enough. (C. Wimber 147)

Lonnie invites the young people forward

Lonnie asked the adults to extend their hands toward the young people and bless them when they came forward, because they would be key to bringing in the harvest. He invited the worship team to play "His Name Is as Ointment Poured Forth."

As they sang through the chorus, Lonnie raised his voice to give instructions. "Everybody stay in an atmosphere of prayer and expect the Spirit of God to move" (Lonnie Frisbee: Mother's Day).

"Everybody twenty-five years old and under come forward… Twenty-five years and younger." The young people rose and started coming to the front.

Carol Wimber comments, "Since that was almost the total congregation, everyone just sort of crowded forward until you couldn't squeeze in sideways" (C. Wimber 147).

In *When the Spirit Comes with Power*, White describes it this way:

> The congregation was predominantly youthful and a large number responded. The speaker waited until they stood before him on the floor of the gymnasium. Older members of the congregation watched, some from chairs on the floor, others from the bleachers. Then he prayed a brief and simple prayer, confessing the Church's failure to give place to the Holy Spirit. He concluded his prayer with the words, "Come, Holy Spirit!" (White 158)

Lonnie invites the Holy Spirit to come

Wimber gives his own account in *Power Evangelism*:

> Then [Lonnie] did something that I had never seen done in a church gathering. He finished his talk and said, "Well, that's my testimony. **Now the church has been offending the Holy Spirit a long time and it is quenched. So we are going to**

invite it to come and minister.[8] We all waited. The air became thick with anticipation—and anxiety.

Then he said, "Holy Spirit, come." And it did!

(I must remind you that we were not a "Pentecostal" church with experience or understanding of the sorts of things that began to happen. What happened could not have been learned behavior.) (Wimber and Springer 24, emphasis mine)

"Ok, adults," Lonnie called, "lay your hands out towards the young people right now. Let's sing it again... Stretch it out towards the young people. Right towards them. Let 'em come! In the midst of the congregation, high praises to Jesus!

"Young people, just hold your hands in a yielding position of availability." To the older folks: "You find a group of young people, and you stretch your hands out towards them. And you take the authority in the name of Jesus, praying with faith, and you begin to believe God to use the young people in this church."

The Holy Spirit moves

Lonnie's tone suddenly became more authoritative. "**There's a tremendous outpouring of the Spirit of God upon the young people here.** The Spirit of the Lord is moving upon these girls here. Lift up your heads, open your eyes. Everybody, keep your eyes open in this. The Spirit of the Lord is moving upon you now in great power. Look at me. I bless you in Jesus' name. Let

---

8   As far as I can tell, the previous two sentences are not found in the actual Mother's Day recording posted on YouTube.

the power and the anointing of the Holy Spirit come on you right here. Let him move on you, my brother, in the name of Jesus, I bless you in his name. Receive the power of God.

"It moves in a chain reaction. Let the Spirit of the Lord move. As the Lord fills you, let the Lord *fill* you, because as the Lord fills *you*, he'll move on others around about you."

Lonnie made his way among the young people, declaring the work of the Spirit with them. "The Spirit of the Lord is moving right here: the girl in the green sweater right here, I bless you in the name of Jesus. Look at me. Let the power of the Holy Spirit come upon your whole body right now. *In Jesus name!*" (Lonnie Frisbee: Mother's Day)

Vineyard historian Bill Jackson recounts:

> The sounds that followed on the tape are now so familiar—the sobbing, bodies vibrating under God's power, loud commands to bless what God was doing, speaking in tongues. Lonnie's voice, trailing away from the microphone as he walked among the fallen youth, continued to invite the Spirit as the fire passed like a daisy chain from one to another. For me these are the sweet sounds of God visiting his people. They were the sounds that accompanied a John Wimber meeting—at least the Wimber meetings *after* 1980. (Jackson, Quest 72–73)

"And now it's on the person next to her," Lonnie exclaimed. "And now on the guy in the blue shirt right here; the Spirit of the Lord is moving in great power. Let the Spirit of the Lord *move over here*! In the name of Jesus, *I bless you in his name*! Receive the anointing and receive the power to be witnesses unto him. Let the power of the Holy Spirit come right here!

"You cannot see the wind," Lonnie declared, "but you can see the leaves as they rustle from the wind. You cannot see the Spirit of God move, but you can see the Spirit of God as he touches people! Right here, let the Spirit of the Lord fill you so he can fill the others.

"I bless you in the name of the Lord. Let the Spirit of the Lord—the power of God is coming on this guy with the cast. Open your eyes. Let the Spirit of the Lord fill you, all through your being, in Jesus' name.

"The guy right here with the braces, keep your eyes open: look, open your eyes, watch, *watch*! This is a class of the Spirit. Open your eyes. The Spirit of the Lord is moving… Let the power of God come. …

"Let the anointing of the Lord *FALL*!" Lonnie shouted. **"Hallelujah, *let the power of the Holy Spirit COME!*"**

Lonnie said, "This is like Pentecost. Let the Spirit of the Lord move over here, let the Spirit of the Lord move over here, in Jesus' name" (Lonnie Frisbee: Mother's Day).

Father, we adore you… Jesus, we adore you… Spirit, we adore you… The worship team continued to play and sing, but they could not drown out the cries of the young people. John Wimber recalls:

> People fell to the floor. Others, who did not believe in tongues, loudly spoke in tongues. The speaker [Lonnie] roamed among the crowd praying for people, who then immediately fell over with the Holy Spirit resting on them. (Wimber and Springer 24)

"Let the Holy Ghost MOVE!" Lonnie shouted under the anointing, wending his way among those slain in the Spirit.[9]

Carol continues, saying that another eyewitness to the meeting claimed:

"The young evangelist was shouting 'More, Lord, more,' and 'Jesus is Lord.'" I was right there and I'm here to tell you that everyone there was shouting, and you couldn't hear anything but the roar of the crowd, as hundreds were filled with the Holy Spirit at the same time and were shouting out loud in tongues. The chairs were falling over and the people were falling on top of the fallen chairs. The leaders that could still function were shouting at one another and it was complete pandemonium. Others were shouting that they were getting out of here. Young Tim Pfeiffer fell face down, pulling the microphone down under him, and if we had ever entertained the thought of keeping any kind of reputation of respectability, it went up to the ceiling of the gymnasium along with Tim's voice—as he shouted uncontrollably in tongues with the volume turned all the way up because someone had crashed into the sound-board. (C. Wimber 147–148)

9   As I listened the recording and transcribed these words during the writing of this book, the Holy Spirit descended on me in power. I shook and wept. If you sense the anointing of God's Spirit upon you as you read this, I encourage you in Jesus' name to pause and receive him, taking as long as you need until he fills you and completes his work.

22. Opinions About the Outpouring

Carol believed that the shaking and other supernatural phenomena that characterized this and future Vineyard meetings was "the transfer of the anointing that was on [founding Quaker] George Fox" (Jackson, Quest 62).

She asked one young man who was laid out on the floor, "What's happening to you right now?" He answered, "It's like electricity. I can't even move!" (74)

Bill Jackson gives the following account of what took place: "The young people were filled with the Spirit, began to fall over, speak in tongues and shake. Witnesses said it looked like a battlefield" (Jackson, Short History).

John White says, "At one point [Lonnie] raised his hand and shouted, 'Jesus is Lord!' and all those facing the palm of his hand fell untidily around the bleachers" (White 158).

Kari Browning, director of New Renaissance Healing & Creativity Center in Post Falls, Idaho, writes: "Lonnie said these now famous words, 'The Church has for years grieved the Holy Spirit, but He's getting over it! Come Holy Spirit!' Hundreds were filled with the Holy Spirit and began to shake and speak in tongues. ... Everyone was in shock, including John Wimber" (Browning).

Bob Fulton, at that time the Yorba Linda youth director (Jackson, Quest 50) and Vineyard church leader, was at the legendary service. He said about 300 young people made their way to the front. When Lonnie said, "Holy Spirit, come," immediately kids started falling to the floor, crying and speaking in tongues. "The sound was shocking," Fulton says. The leaders had no idea what to do. Many people got up and left. Some were angry (Di Sabatino).

Carol Wimber tells us what her husband was doing when the Holy Ghost fell:

> John was paralysed, caught in mid-motion as he reached for the mike, and I couldn't tell if that look on his face was profound wonder or sheer terror. Others and myself started wading through the fallen bodies assessing the situation. I met John somewhere in the pile and **I told him I thought it was the Lord. After all, hadn't we been praying for power for ministry?** This, John, was it! He gazed at me with a sort of stunned, faraway expression.
>
> John's senses were still functioning, though, no matter how deeply in shock he was, because he heard very clearly the Bibles slam shut and saw just as clearly those same people stomp furiously out of the gym, some never to be seen by us again. I know we repopulated the Friends Church with horrified ex-Vineyard members. That's fine. It's only fair. (C. Wimber 148, emphasis mine)

Wimber struggles with the outpouring

Fulton said Wimber took a lot of backlash from this outpouring under Lonnie's ministry (Di Sabatino). Wimber himself confessed,

I was aghast! All I could think throughout the experience was, "Oh, God, get me out of here." In the aftermath, we lost church members and my staff was extremely upset. That night I could not sleep. Instead, I spent the evening reading Scripture, looking for the verse, "Holy Spirit, come." I never found it. (Wimber and Springer 25)

White shares the following about Wimber's struggle.

But a deeper doubt haunted his bedroom. It was evident that an extraordinary source of power had invaded the gymnasium. What was its nature? Where had it come from? Was it merely the result of immature judgment on the part of an impulsive young man? The word *pandemonium* (which seemed to describe what had happened) has to do with demons. Was it evil? Could it be of God? (White 159)

Wimber received an unexpected telephone call from pastor Tom Stipe, who had a three-word message from God for him: "That was me!" (160) According to Carol Wimber:

[John] stayed up with his books on church history and revivals and studied and prayed. About five in the morning, Tommy Stipe called from Denver. "I don't know what's going on there, John, but the Lord woke me and told me to call and tell you that it's him. Does that make sense?" God bless Tom Stipe! (C. Wimber 148)

Wimber eventually overcame his apprehensions, accepting the Mother's Day outpouring as a move of God. In *Power Evangelism* he gives his version of the Stipe call:

I asked God for assurance that this was from him, that this was something he—not humans or Satan—was doing. Just after praying this prayer, the phone rang. Tom Stipe, a Denver, Colorado, pastor and good friend, called. I told him what had happened the night before, and he responded that it was from God. "That's exactly what happened in the early days of the Jesus People revival. Many people were saved." That conversation was significant, because Tom was a credible witness. I had only heard about these things; Tom had lived through them. (Wimber and Springer 25)

When God delivers the unexpected

Psychiatrist John White asks, "Why do many people who pray earnestly for a visitation from God reject what he sends because they find it offensive?" (White 33)

Wimber had been seeking God for a visitation of his presence. Yet when it came, it wasn't what he expected. Perhaps this is why churches don't see more of the miraculous in their midst: they don't want the mess that comes with revival.

At a meeting of church elders a few days later, Lonnie told Wimber that *Wimber* needed to have an encounter with God, and Wimber ended up on the floor, under the power of the Holy Spirit (Di Sabatino).

23. The Results of the Outpouring

What were the results of this fateful outpouring on Mother's Day? Some eyewitnesses of the aftermath share their news and views.

Vineyard staff initially upset

Carol Wimber reveals that the next morning, John went to their offices at Wagner House, where an unhappy staff were already waiting for him.

> He met first of all with the associate and his wife, and I'll never forget what he said. He listened to their complaints (legitimate complaints: they'd been up all night too), until they were through, and then he removed his glasses and leaned forward and spoke very softly, but very clearly. "I understand how you feel. What happened last night may result in people leaving, but there is something you need to understand about me if we are to continue to work together. If ever there is a choice between the smart thing to do and the move of the Holy Spirit, I will always land on the side of the Spirit. You need to know that." It was a defining moment in the Vineyard, and it's etched indelibly in my memory. (C. Wimber 148, emphasis mine)

Revival breaks out among youth

Carol continues with brighter news:

Our church was somewhat altered by that outpouring of the Spirit. As I said, we never again saw many of the people that stormed out that night, **but a revival broke out among the young people and they took it to the school campuses in the area, and Bible studies started popping up all over the place.** Attendance grew along with the conversions and we probably hit two thousand about that time. (C. Wimber 149, emphasis mine)

Bob Fulton's daughter was in junior high then, and "The young people at her school who belonged to their church began to **witness with great power on the campus. Kids began repenting of their sins** and some were so overcome by the Spirit's presence that they could no longer stand up" (Jackson, Quest 75).

Other positive results of the outpouring are summarized here:

The young kids, many in junior high and high school, were so "filled with the Spirit" that they soon started baptizing friends in hot tubs and swimming pools around town. The church catapulted in growth over the next few months and the event is credited with launching the Vineyard Movement. After this time, Frisbee and Wimber began traveling the world, visiting South Africa and Europe. ... While there, they performed many healings and miracles for people. As reported by many who were there, Frisbee was integral to the development of what would later become Wimber's "signs and wonders theology." (Lonnie Frisbee: Wikipedia, emphasis mine)

The birth of signs and wonders

Mother's Day 1980, according to Bill Jackson, "proved to be a seminal event in that it birthed the reality of power evangelism and confirmed for John Wimber his original thesis that the church can grow exponentially when accompanied by signs and wonders. Power evangelism launched the 'Vineyard' that was in John's heart" (Jackson, Quest 344).

In his appendixed essay in Jackson's *The Quest for the Radical Middle*, David Di Sabatino provides the account of an unnamed pastor who, sometime *after* the Mother's Day outpouring, invited Lonnie to come and minister in his church.

> After Frisbee took the stage and announced, "Come, Holy Spirit!" the pastor related that the events that followed were "exceedingly difficult to describe." He stated, "**within seconds the Spirit of God had fallen upon a large proportion of the congregation**, many of whom were trembling and shaking, speaking in tongues, calling on the Lord, prophesying, and some of whom (hard though it might seem to believe) were flapping up and down like fish upon the floor. Some of this I was able to see, but most of it passed me by since I was doing the same." In his estimation **Frisbee was the "trigger" for an emphasis on spiritual phenomena in those early years within the Vineyard movement.** (387, emphasis mine)

In 1982 Wimber and C. Peter Wagner launched a course at Fuller Theological Seminary called "The Miraculous and Church Growth." The course included hands-on training in signs, wonders, and healing. The Holy Spirit regularly manifested in these classes.

Missions afire

Lonnie's ministry also set fire to the Vineyard's missions efforts. Jackson claims, "The history of missions in the Vineyard actually began through the ministry of Lonnie Frisbee" (241). And it started even before the Mother's Day meeting.

David Owen was a South African pastor who had started a fellowship in Johannesburg as part of a church-planting movement called "The Invisible Church." Young people who wanted God to build a new wineskin for the fullness of his power for their generation formed this network of churches.

Jackson explains that an American missionary recommended Owen invite Lonnie Frisbee to minister. At that time, Lonnie was attending Wimber's church, which was still associated with Calvary Chapel. Owen brought Lonnie to South Africa that same year (242). Jackson describes what happened:

> On the first night of meetings, the Spirit of God visited David's congregation mightily. They started at six o'clock and were still going strong at eleven. People were being healed, saved, delivered, shaken, and empowered. David says that the presence of God was awesome. He was so touched that he went over to America to spend some time in Wimber's church in March of 1980 and left to return to South Africa at the end of April. Just before he left, he spoke at the church, which numbered about 500 people at the time. It was the very next week that Lonnie Frisbee gave his testimony at the evening service at Canyon High School and Wimber's church was catapulted into revival.
>
> When David came back to Anaheim in July, the church had mushroomed in attendance. Wimber writes in *Power*

Evangelism that **between May and September they baptized over 700 new converts with estimates that there may have been as many as 1,700 that prayed to receive Christ**. During this period David Owen's church officially aligned with John's.

John and Carol Wimber went to South Africa in October 1980 and brought with them a team comprised of Lonnie, Kenn Gulliksen, John and Margie McClure, and two laymen. They did a series of meetings on church growth for pastors during the day and had open meetings at night. The power of God was visibly evident.

David remembers one incident in particular. It was late, and Lonnie was very tired, having prayed for people all night. He stopped to pray for one last woman in her fifties who was completely blind. Her sight was restored instantly, and she began shouting in jubilation, telling everyone what clothes they were wearing. The woman worked for an important company associated with the mining industry, and the story was written up in their company newsletter. The *Sunday Times*, the largest newspaper in the country, also did a spread on her, thus giving God glory and Wimber instant credibility. (242–243, emphasis mine)

Wimber got the credit, but it was Lonnie who had gone the second mile to pray for the woman. Wherever Lonnie went, the Holy Spirit manifested.

After the Yorba Linda church separated from Calvary Chapel in 1982, Wimber took a team of seventy-two people from all over the U.S. to South Africa. Owen had started a new Vineyard church with fifty people, and with Wimber's team they all hit the streets of Johannesburg to evangelize, inviting those to whom they ministered to attend the evening meetings.

A former roommate of Lonnie's, Marwan Bahu, was on the trip and remembers: "**One evening when Lonnie prayed for God to come, every one of the 500 or so people (excluding the ministry team) fell out under the power of God.** The ministry team left the building because God was apparently doing quite well without them" (246, emphasis mine).

24. The Vineyard Flourishes

Another result of the Mother's Day outpouring was that Calvary Chapel, Yorba Linda, split from its parent organization and joined a different stream that also had its roots in Calvary.

Kenn Gulliksen, founder of the Vineyard

Kenn Gulliksen and his wife Joanie were part of Calvary Chapel, Costa Mesa, in the early 1970s, and Kenn was ordained at Calvary in 1971.

After a stint in Texas, the Gulliksens returned to Los Angeles to plant a church. Jackson reveals, "He fully intended to remain within the network of Calvary relationships, but he sensed the Lord doing something a bit different" (Jackson, Quest 78).

Gulliksen considered the Vineyard to be similar to Calvary, but with "more emphasis on intimacy in worship, the gifts of the Spirit, and relationships" (80).

Gulliksen started Bible studies in the homes of musicians Chuck Girard and Larry Norman, meeting corporately on Sundays at the Beverly Hills Women's Club. Musician Keith Green came to faith in Christ through the Gulliksens' Beverly Hills Bible study. Keith and his wife Melody went on to found Last Days Ministries (80).

Di Sabatino shares that Kenn Gulliksen credits Frisbee with "mentoring him in the 'deeper things' of the Holy Spirit" (379).

Chuck Smith, however, disagreed with teaching "truth" based on subjective experiences—his basic conflict with Lonnie's ministry. Gulliksen believed Smith had "an aversion to the hype and manipulation that he had experienced in the Foursquare churches of his generation." So when John Wimber began to "promote in the front room what Calvary was doing only in the back room, tension began to mount" (83).

In April 1982 Smith invited Calvary Chapel branch pastors to a meeting for fellowship and prayer. Among those who attended were Mike MacIntosh (pastor of Horizon Christian Fellowship in San Diego), Greg Laurie, John Wimber, and Kenn Gulliksen. Some pastors, says Jackson, "were upset with John's new emphasis on the Holy Spirit and his use of church growth principles that seemed to contradict Chuck's teaching on the sovereignty of God in the expansion of the church." To solve the problem, they suggested Wimber's church align with the Vineyard, which had grown to six in number, under Gulliksen's leadership.

The Vineyard branches off from Calvary Chapel

Wimber and Gulliksen started plans to affiliate (83-84). Not long afterward, the leadership of the new Vineyard shifted. Jackson explains:

> Kenn, a man of genuine vision, knew that the Lord had great plans for the Vineyard, but he also knew his own limitations. John, with all his experience in church growth, had the skills and willingness to pastor and train leaders. Kenn, therefore, felt led of the Lord to submit the Vineyard to John's leadership (84).

Yet at that time, Gulliksen says Chuck Smith did not foresee the Vineyard branch separating from the Calvary Chapel root, but only as having a "different flavor." Between 1974 and 1982, all of the Vineyard fellowships were full partners with Calvary. However, there were key differences between the Vineyard and the traditional Calvary churches. Vineyard historian Bill Jackson points out the following distinctions:

- John Wimber realized that with his new theological convictions he was not a good fit in the Calvary system.
- Kenn Gulliksen "wanted to pursue intimacy with Christ, and Vineyard worship reflected this more intimate approach."
- Gulliksen also developed a ministry of inner healing, which Wimber would share, but Calvary did not.
- Much of the Vineyard's growth came from evangelicals wanting more of the Holy Spirit's power in their lives.
- Calvary held as a central doctrine the pre-tribulational, imminent return of Christ. (Chuck Smith predicted the rapture would occur in 1981. It did not.) Wimber developed a post-tribulational position from the theology of George Ladd.
- The Vineyard entered deliverance ministry for believers, while Chuck Smith maintained that "no Christian will ever be in need of deliverance" (85–87).

As Calvary hit their stride as a church-planting movement, according to Jackson, "the Vineyard rose up to represent a more aggressive affirmation of the present-day ministry of the Holy Spirit" (39). Eventually, thirty churches formerly associated with Calvary Chapel affiliated with the Vineyard.

In 1982 Wimber's church changed its name to the Anaheim Vineyard Christian Fellowship (Association of Vineyard Churches). Although it remained evangelical, from that time the Vineyard took on a stronger Pentecostal practice (Di Sabatino).

In years previous, says White, Wimber "was confronted with the fact that in opposing 'supernatural' manifestations he might have been opposing God" (White 160). Although Wimber gradually turned away from his former cessationist beliefs, **what happened during Lonnie's ministry was the catalyst for a complete about-face.** Wimber explains the results of the Mother's Day outpouring:

> Over the next few months, supernatural phenomena continued to occur, frequently uninvited and without any encouragement, spontaneously. **New life came into our church.** All who were touched by and who yielded to the Holy Spirit—whether they fell over, started shaking, became very quiet and still, or spoke in tongues—accepted the experience and thought it was wonderful, drawing them closer to God. **More importantly, prayer, Scripture reading, caring for others, and the love of God all increased.**
>
> **Our young people went out into the community, looking for people to evangelize and pray over.** An event that I heard about is a good illustration of what often happened. One day a group of our young people approached a stranger in a parking lot. Soon they were praying over him, and he fell to the ground. By the time he got up, the stranger was converted. He is now a member of our church.
>
> **A revival began that May, and by September we had baptized over seven hundred new converts.** There may have

been as many as seventeen hundred new converts during a three-and-a-half-month period. I was an expert on church growth, but I had never seen evangelism like that.

Power encounters in the church, in this case without regard for "civilized propriety," catapulted us into all-out revival. (Wimber and Springer 26, emphasis mine)

The Vineyard rejects TACF

D. Martyn Lloyd-Jones believes, "If your doctrine of the Holy Spirit does not include this idea of the Holy Spirit falling upon people, it is seriously, grievously defective" (Lloyd-Jones 115–116). Yet, fourteen years later, when the Holy Spirit fell at the Toronto Airport Vineyard Church (TACF) in 1994 during a series of meetings with visiting pastor Randy Clark, the tables turned.

> Some religious leaders criticized the church and revival because of the teachings and manifestations that occurred. Wimber initially defended the Airport Vineyard saying, "Nearly everything we've seen—falling, weeping, laughing, shaking—has been seen before, not only in our own memory, but in revivals all over the world." (Maxwell 38)

But in a *Christianity Today* interview, Wimber later said that the Toronto revival was "changing our definition of renewal in Vineyard" and that the Vineyard decided to "withdraw endorsement." TACF resigned from the Vineyard (Stafford and Beverley).

Lonnie's influence on the Vineyard

Did Lonnie's anointing bring a move of the Spirit to the Calvary Chapel and Vineyard ministries? Carol Wimber shares her opinion about what happened on Mother's Day.

> [I]t would be easier to say that the power came with Lonnie, but the truth is that the power of the Holy Spirit was breaking out in all the groups, even before Lonnie came to the church. Certainly not on such a widespread scale, though. I think that it was just that **he knew what to do when the Spirit was there and most of us didn't**. After I met him a few years before at the pastors' retreat, I had gone down to the beach area near Calvary Chapel, just to go to a Bible study he was teaching, but there was no particular presence of God. He ministered in a vague sort of way to a few people, but nothing much was happening then. In reality, he walked into a move of God here in Yorba Linda and had the faith or moxie or know-how to move with it. He could "see" the Spirit on people, but he didn't bring the Holy Spirit with him. (C. Wimber 149, emphasis mine)

Jackson believes that during Wimber's Fuller years, many factors besides Lonnie's ministry converged to develop his signs and wonders theology (Jackson, Quest).

Lonnie was with the Vineyard for only a few years. But many say his catalyst launched the Vineyard into a multi-church movement that spread just as Calvary Chapel had. Within six months of the Mother's Day meeting, Kathy Baldock claims, "Wimber's Vineyard church, with the help of Frisbee's preaching, teaching, and praying, exploded from 500 to 2,500 in attendance" (Baldock, Walking the Bridgeless Canyon 355).

Di Sabatino says Lonnie "played a crucial role in the rocketing advance of both Calvary Chapel and the Vineyard" (Jackson, Quest 377).

> Though little credit is given to Lonnie, he was influential in the formation of what the Vineyard church movement called "the signs and wonders theology," a paradigm of teaching that suggests that all Christians could operate in a similar manner to Lonnie—that they too could perform miracles like they'd read in the New Testament (Di Sabatino).

"An anointed person is recognized by the power and presence of God upon their life," says Di Sabatino. But rejection begins when people believe such a one has sinned.

25. Lonnie Ousted from Vineyard Because of Homosexuality

Lonnie had participated in the gay scene in Laguna Beach and San Francisco as a teenager, before his conversion. At the end of his marriage to Connie and after their divorce, he returned to it. Yet he loved the Lord, and the Holy Spirit confirmed his preaching with signs, wonders, and miracles. What was going on?

Many at that time, including Lonnie, felt that a true conversion to Christ would "deliver" anyone from homosexuality. But did God change Lonnie's orientation simply because he was saved and baptized with the Holy Spirit?

Waiting at the door

In his autobiography, Lonnie shares about a close relationship he had with a young man he calls Blair, whom he met on a mission trip to Europe. Although Lonnie *does not* share anything more than their spiritual relationship, his language is telling.

> When we arrived back from the mission a special bonding had taken place, like if you had gone on an exciting hunting trip, except we had been fishing for men. Blair and I decided that we would seek the Lord early in the morning every other day. Now, I normally didn't get up at 5:30 a.m., but I would

drive from Newport Beach… to Blair's place in Huntington Beach.

> I would arrive and Blair would have hot herbal tea all prepared. It was the first time that I ever drank herbal tea. He would be waiting for me at the door with a hot cup each morning. … [W]hen Blair and I began to seek the Lord's face, immediately the power of the Holy Spirit lifted us up into spheres of light. There was no doubt that both of us were experiencing the same thing! (Frisbee and Sachs 127–129)

What kind of closeness beyond spiritual fellowship developed between Lonnie and Blair remains unknown, but in Di Sabatino's documentary, Chuck Smith Jr reveals that an unnamed young man confessed to the pastor of a Laguna Beach church that he'd had a six-month affair with Lonnie.

Smith questioned John Wimber about it. Wimber confronted Lonnie, who was still at his church, and Lonnie admitted the affair.

Lonnie sidelined and then ousted

Vineyard pulled Lonnie out of visible ministry and put more and more boundaries on him. These strictures ostensibly failed. They eventually let him go.

Di Sabatino explains that after Lonnie left the Vineyard in 1983, with no church affiliation he traveled as an itinerant evangelist to South Africa and South America, experiencing missionary success but also suffering depression (Jackson, Quest 387).

Was Lonnie the harbinger of Holy Spirit revival or the "wolf at the door" he had warned Carol Wimber about? We'll consider next what others said about him.

26. Reactions to Lonnie's Orientation

Connie Bremer-Murray confided to Di Sabatino that when Lonnie asked her to marry him, he told her he was gay. "He didn't say it as though he was still gay," she clarified, "but that he had been saved out of that lifestyle."

Was Lonnie a "practicing homosexual"?

Those who were close to Lonnie believed he had renounced homosexuality at his conversion and that he always maintained it was a sin. Friend and one-time roommate John Ruttkay said Lonnie may have lapsed at times, but was not a practicing homosexual.

Yet Lonnie engaged in sexual activity with men at several points throughout his life. Lonnie's homosexuality was a lifelong struggle that "did not go away with his profession of faith in Jesus Christ" (Di Sabatino).

Steve Toth, hippie Christian, found it hard to understand that Lonnie could party on Saturday night and preach on Sunday morning when "the Spirit of God moved, and there was no doubt about it" (Di Sabatino).

Kent Philpott admits, "I did not know until years after his death from AIDS that [Lonnie] had ever been involved homosexuality. He never once talked about it with me nor did anyone at the House of Acts mention it to me" (Philpott 63).

Reactions to Lonnie's behavior

Di Sabatino reveals what resulted from the discovery of Lonnie's homosexuality by Calvary and the Vineyard: "Because conservative Christians look upon sexual sins as being more grievous than other indiscretions, Lonnie was branded an outcast and treated with contempt by those he had helped establish in the ministry." Elsewhere he states,

> While close friends attested that he rarely (if ever) exhibited any indication that he was struggling in this area of his life, **his death as a result of AIDS has been interpreted by many as an outright indictment of flagrant licentiousness unbecoming of a Christian minister** (Jackson, Quest 388, emphasis mine).

John White identifies our "you-can't-have-it-both-ways mentality" when it comes to the Holy Spirit manifesting through someone deemed a moral failure. "Either the power is of God, and therefore the person exercising it must be pleasing to God, or else the person is displeasing God and the power (if it is real) must be from the pit [of hell]" (White 125).

This attitude is reminiscent of the colorful opinion R. A. Torrey spouted about Pentecostalism in 1907. When a San Antonio newspaper reported that the movement's instigator, Charles Fox Parham, was accused (falsely) of having had relations with a man (Cauchi), Torrey broad-brushed the entire movement as "emphatically not of God and founded by a sodomite" (Synan 146).[10]

Vineyard leader Bob Fulton, who experienced the Spirit's outpouring on Mother's Day, admits they felt remorse because "we let somebody that was a practicing homosexual minister, and we didn't know it" (Di Sabatino).

Brant Baker's story

Like Lonnie, Brant Baker was a young charismatic minister who also came out of the Jesus Movement and was a devotee of Kathryn Kuhlman's.

Baker was saved in a Billy Graham Crusade in San Diego at the age of sixteen. He attended Calvary Chapel during the years when young people flocked there, apparently when Lonnie Frisbee was ministering. He learned the Bible from Chuck Smith.

When his grandmother was hospitalized with a stroke, Baker went to the ICU and "laid his hands on her and began interceding. What he [described] as the Shekinah glory filled the room and his grandmother's miraculous healing began." (Sloane, Shekinah)

A teaching opportunity opened up in Long Beach, and David Sloane describes what happened in these early meetings:

> Each Saturday evening a handful of teenagers gathered to hear Brant teach lengthy Bible studies. A time of worship followed and special prayer was made for those desiring healing or baptism in the Holy Spirit. Miraculous recoveries from a variety of illnesses became a common part of these meetings. (Sloane, Shekinah)

---

10 For a discussion about this broad-brushing attitude toward homosexuality and the religious terminology used to condemn it, see *The Sin of Sodom: What the Bible Really Teaches About Why God Destroyed the Cities of the Plain* (Acceptable Books, 2015).

The fledgling group expanded and moved to a larger church facility, which became Shekinah Fellowship. As the congregation of young people grew, they changed venues, eventually ending up at Long Beach Neighborhood Four-square Church in 1973. (Its pastor, Rev. Billy Adams, had been acquainted personally with Aimee Semple McPherson.)

Church services included the ministry of healing, which included laying hands on the sick and Baker calling out healings by the word of knowledge, like Kuhlman.

By December 1973, the Saturday night meetings in the Long Beach Foursquare Church were filled to capacity. Eleven months had passed since Brant Baker had begun services in the new facilities and approximately one thousand people attended each week. A 90-voice choir became a part of the ministry, along with an orchestra and two singing groups. Miracles of healing had increased tremendously, with some cases of cancer, blindness and similarly hopeless diseases and conditions being cured instantly during the meetings. (Sloane, Shekinah)

A video of a Shekinah Fellowship service with Baker preaching is available on YouTube.[11]

The ministry continued to swell, and in fulfillment of a revelation given to Baker, they held a revival service at Angelus Temple, the massive facility built by McPherson.

On July 4, 1974, the all-day Holy Ghost Rally at Angelus Temple concluded with a divine healing service conducted by Rev. Baker and Shekinah Fellowship. The same group that had

---

11   https://www.youtube.com/watch?v=c8qknVXGPeY.

begun two years earlier in a living room was now ministering in the headquarters of the International Church of the Foursquare Gospel (Sloane, Shekinah).

Shekinah held monthly services at Angelus Temple and also traveled to other cities holding crusades. Baker appeared on Trinity Broadcasting Network. It seemed there was no end to the increase of Shekinah Fellowship's outreach.

But Brant Baker's ministry crashed when it was discovered that he was gay. Like Lonnie, he was quickly purged from the history books. Both Brant and his brother Kevin Baker, also gay, died of AIDS (Sloane, Shekinah).

An anonymous writer who contributed a memory of Baker from his ministry days had this to say about being present when Baker received a phone call. Baker said into the phone:

"No, not Lonnie!", and for some strange reason I just intuitively knew he was talking about Lonnie being gay, although at that point no one, not even I knew, that Brant was gay, or Lonnie.

I had taken my friend Kevin Laubach to a service at the Vineyard and he got really angry. It was the night that Lonnie called all the young people to come down. Kevin's emotion was so strong and it was because he could tell Lonnie was gay, and told me so. He thought it was a sham. (Sloane, People Speak)

Despite Lonnie and Brant being gay, the Holy Spirit moved through these young men to save and heal countless people, yet many still believe their ministry was a sham.

The recent history of homosexuality in the U.S.

Much history led to this point. For centuries, the church condemned *any* form of sex that was not procreative, including heterosexual sex between married couples.

The modern concept of "homosexuality" didn't appear until 1868. It wasn't until 1934 that both the words "homosexuality" and "heterosexuality" appeared in *Webster's Dictionary*. World War II changed national gender roles with a significant number of women entering the workforce.

The advent of psychoanalysis, poorly conducted research, and the theories based on it—such as those of Sigmund Freud, Edmund Bergler, Sandor Rado, Lionel Ovesy, Irving Biebler, and Charles Socarides—usually did more harm than good to gays and lesbians in the first three-quarters of the twentieth century. The unified opinion of these so-called "experts" resulted in not only the medical community but all of society, including the church, viewing homosexuality as pathological—a mental disorder (Baldock, Walking the Bridgeless Canyon 53).

Newsman Mike Wallace produced a 1967 *CBS Reports* documentary that revealed the results of a CBS News survey stating,

> Two out of three Americans look upon homosexuals with disgust, discomfort, or fear. One out of ten says "hatred." A vast majority believes that homosexuality is an illness; only 10% say it is a crime. And yet, and here's the paradox, the majority of Americans favor legal punishment, even for homosexual acts performed in private, between consenting adults.

In fact, narrates Wallace, "Americans consider homosexuality more harmful to society than adultery, abortion, or prostitution" (CBS Reports).

Researcher Alfred Kinsey's reports on male and female sexuality (1948 and 1953) let Americans know just what was going on in everyone's bedrooms, and it wasn't as wholesome as everyone had thought. Fearing the dissolution of society at the hands of communists and sexual perverts, at mid-century, America passed and enforced new sex-crime laws. The penalty for being found out a homosexual included arrest, loss of job, or institutionalization, where treatment such as lobotomy or electroshock therapy was routinely administered.

After the publication of the groundless Hoey Committee report in 1950, thousands of U.S. government workers were fired for proof—and even on the suspicion of—being gay. President Eisenhower signed Executive Order 10450, "The Security Requirements for Government Employment," in 1953 to ensure national security, keeping anyone with questionable morals or sexuality out of federal employ (Baldock, Walking the Bridgeless Canyon 16–78).

The intersection of hippies and homosexuality

This was the environment that older church leaders and even Lonnie Frisbee had been raised in. If greater society was this strict even into the 1960s and 70s, you can be sure it was stricter in the church.

This history puts not only homosexuality, but "free love" hippies, into perspective. It was at the end of this time that God poured out his Spirit on the disillusioned and disenfranchised young people of America.

Kathy Baldock states, "Three major church movements—Calvary Chapel, the Vineyard, and Harvest Christian Fellowship—were birthed as part of the Southern California Jesus Movement. **The intersection, commonality, and key to the massive explosion of all three was one man: Lonnie Frisbee**" (349–350, emphasis mine).

"There is no mention of how influential Lonnie was over the growth of the Calvary Chapel or Vineyard Church movements," says Di Sabatino, "both of which have grown into worldwide denominations, each with more than 1000 ˊchurches" (Di Sabatino).

Is Lonnie honored for his role in America's greatest revival? I love him, but many Christians don't.

Was Lonnie written out of church history?

Philpott reports, "I heard from people who were close to Lonnie at the time, that a kind of jealousy developed, primarily over Lonnie's notoriety, and an attempt was made to curtail the characteristic independence that Lonnie clung to."

After the conflict and breaks with Chuck Smith and Calvary and then John Wimber and the Vineyard, Philpott believes that Lonnie essentially was "thrown under the bus" (Philpott 64). In *Memoirs of a Jesus Freak*, Philpott marks this statement with a footnote:

> I have struggled over this somewhat harsh treatment of fellow Christians, but I thought it necessary to tell it like I saw it or the account of Lonnie Frisbee would be incomplete or appear doctored to please others (64).

Former pastor David Hayward concurs. "I realize that [Di Sabatino's] documentary in many ways is sympathetic to Lonnie Frisbee and critical of those who rejected him. However, this has been my observation about the church as well. It is no surprise. It is disturbing but predictable. What more can be said?" Yet, he asserts, "[E]ven though the Vineyard has written him out of our history, he is a part of our foundational roots. The issue of being gay in the church is a very real issue today" (Hayward).

Lonnie was let go and many, including Hayward and Di Sabatino, claim that he was "written out of church history," qualified as being unworthy to be used by God. Yet both Calvary Chapel and the Vineyard received thousands of members reaped from genuine conversions because of the anointing of the Holy Spirit on Lonnie. Long-time friend Ken Fish says, "Lonnie was not wise enough to understand that people constantly wanted to use him for his anointing and throw him away as a human being" (Di Sabatino).

Bob Fulton denies that Lonnie was written out of Vineyard history. "We'll admit that God used Lonnie Frisbee to do certain things to us, and we're not ashamed of that" (Di Sabatino). Yet John Wimber refers to Lonnie during that watershed Mother's Day meeting in *Power Evangelism* only as "the young man" and "the speaker."

In an article covering the release of Di Sabatino's documentary, *Frisbee: The Life and Death of a Hippie Preacher*, the KQED Arts department published this:

Besides the dynamic influence that Frisbee had over the lives of countless individuals, and beyond the miraculous stories that swirl in the wake of his life, what makes the story most fascinating is that **God called Lonnie Frisbee while he was deeply involved in the homosexual lifestyle in Laguna Beach, California. Because of this, however, his spiritual mentors were always skittish about involving him in their ministries even though they could not deny the influence and dramatic results that occurred whenever Lonnie was around.** After his death in 1993 from AIDS, he was basically stricken from the written record of those ministries. At his funeral he was eulogized as the biblical character Samson, a man of great spiritual strength whose personal frailties ultimately got the best of him.

The documentary tells the story of a simple man whom God empowered to fulfill a grand purpose, and who suffered the mistreatment of his spiritual overseers because of his honesty and his struggles. **For anyone who has suffered the abuses of organized religion but still wants to hold on to faith, Lonnie Frisbee's life is a testament that God still finds favor among the regular everyday people.** (Frisbee: KQED, emphasis mine)

In an interview published in *Christianity Today*, David Di Sabatino reveals, "Both the Calvary Chapel people and the Vineyard people have come back to me to point to books where Lonnie's been mentioned, but I'm careful to say in the movie that his influence has not been properly contextualized. I don't think putting his name in one of the lines in a book means anything. **There was a concerted effort not to talk about Lonnie**" (Chattaway, emphasis mine).

Blogger Kenny Petrowski shares his perspective about the downplaying of Lonnie's role:

The piece about Lonnie being left out of Vineyard history…
is just untrue. Yes, in *Power Evangelism* Wimber refers to
Lonnie as "the young man,"[12] so I can see where there could
be some foul play there, BUT in all the other published docu-
ments (the two that I know of), Lonnie is talked about, sometimes in detail:

- In *The Way it Was*, Carol Wimber shares about Lonnie by
  name (and that book is not meant to be a Vineyard history,
  but rather a book about John).
- In *The Quest for the Radical Middle* there is a whole chapter all about Lonnie, his life and his impact on the Vineyard.[13]

According to our friends, … I understand that the Vineyard
leaders made sure Lonnie was financially ok and didn't screw
him when removing him from a very public platform. That
they took care of business as need be (but with grace for him
as friend and individual). If you watch Lonnie's memorial
service on Google Video, it appears that Wimber had
contributed something (I don't know if that was friendship,
financially or what) towards him very late in his life (per
some of the comments made). (Petrowski)

Theologian and author Tony Jones at *Theoblogy*, commenting on Di Sabatino's documentary, remarks:

---

12 Vineyard historian Bill Jackson reports that Kevin Springer actually
    wrote *Power Evangelism* from Wimber's Fuller lecture notes and tapes,
    with Wimber only revising "each chapter as he saw fit" (Jackson, Quest
    109).

13 Lonnie is mentioned briefly in a chapter, but the largest segment in
    Jackson's book devoted to Lonnie is actually an appendix (III) written
    by David Di Sabatino.

I couldn't help but be reminded of Max Weber's definition that *charisma* is, "a certain quality of an individual personality, by virtue of which he is set apart from ordinary men and treated as endowed with supernatural, superhuman, or at least specifically exceptional powers or qualities. These are such as are not accessible to the ordinary person, but are regarded as of divine origin or as exemplary, and on the basis of them the individual concerned is treated as a leader." **That's Lonnie Frisbee in a nutshell.**

More damning, however, is Weber's conclusion that **religious charisma is *always* routinized and bureaucratized as the generation that follows the charismatic leader attempts to capture the charisma and make a living from it**. And *that* is Calvary Chapel and the Vineyard. (Jones, emphasis mine)

Evangelist and pastor of Harvest Christian Fellowship, Greg Laurie, laments in his biography *Lost Boy* that he wished he'd had a more clean-cut conversion and upbringing in the Lord.

When I reflected on my story of faith, I thought, Why couldn't I have been led to Christ by someone I admired as much as Billy Graham? That would have been something I could be proud of....

But no. **I was introduced to Christ by Lonnie Frisbee; one of the most controversial and charismatic figures of his day.**

... Lonnie went off track. As Chuck Smith put it later, with much love and regret, he became "spiritually sterile." Perhaps that was why he succumbed to a spiral of temptations that ultimately resulted in him contracting the AIDS virus. (Laurie and Vaughn 138, emphasis mine)

The results of rejection

Matt Coker states that Lonnie's ex-wife Connie Bremer-Murray championed Di Sabatino's documentary, which argues that Lonnie sparked the huge growth of the Calvary and Vineyard church movements in Orange County during the 1970s, "yet he's at best a historical footnote because he struggled with homosexuality and died of AIDS in 1993" (Coker, Ears on Their Head).

Rev. Samuel Kader writes, "When the topic of sexuality hits the church there are few or no answers that work." Instead,

There are platitudes. There are plenty of traditional theologies based on scriptural interpretations. But when those traditions fail, the person seeking help is considered a moral failure and asked to leave. The *tradition* is never questioned. The tradition declares that all non-heterosexual orientations are evil and must be changed. This tradition, however, has never brought freedom. It has brought bondage, legalism, ostracism, depression, psychiatric institutional admissions, despondency, and suicide. It has driven people from God and the church and offered no hope. (Kader 9)

Lonnie did become depressed. But he never gave up on God. After being let go from the Vineyard, he broke ties with churches and began independent missions work in foreign nations, where he enjoyed a fruitful ministry he mentions in *Not By Might Nor By Power.*

27. Lonnie's Death

Lonnie had a difficult upbringing marred by violence and abuse. He took drugs. He naturally acted on his orientation as a gay teenager. He dropped out of art school, became a hippie, and explored all kind of counterculture spirituality.

But he accepted Christ, was baptized in the Holy Spirit, studied the Word, and spent himself on reaching the lost and equipping the church. He married and divorced. He did other things he and his mentors considered to be sinful.

Weighing Lonnie's life

Does the bad overshadow the good? Do Lonnie's mistakes invalidate his successes? How could God have used him? Unless, of course, his ministry was a complete sham because of his failures.

At the end of his life, what did Lonnie think? In answer to why he thought God used him in such powerful ways, Lonnie states in his autobiography:

> I stand in total awe every time the Lord touches our lives, every time He reveals His loving kindness toward us. Every time He uses me. Believe me, I am the least likely candidate for what the Lord has done with me. I look back and the only explanation I can offer is that since I was a little child, I have desperately needed God. I had nothing or no one to turn to

except God. He responded to my cries with a plan and a divine purpose for my life. (Frisbee and Sachs 14)

Lonnie's demise

Lonnie visited the doctor in the early 1990s, and a blood test revealed he had contracted HIV. Within four months he developed AIDS. Lonnie was ashamed of this. But he loved the Lord and served God until the end. He found forgiveness and made peace with many of his former associates in ministry, forgiving "all those who had ostracized him and shunned him in the past" (Crowder).

Lonnie Ray Frisbee died on March 12, 1993, at the age of 43.

Bittersweet remembrances

Church-planter and former Vineyard leader Steve Sjogren has this to say about Lonnie:

Few people have had more impact on the 20th[-century] church scene in the west than a little known guy named Lonnie Frisbee. Like a lot of change makers, he was controversial, and sadly, he died pretty much penniless and with few steadfast friends, yet God chose to use this guy in amazing ways. (Sjogren)

Mega-church pastor Greg Laurie visited Lonnie in his final days and shares this account in *Lost Boy*:

My friend Mike MacIntosh and I went to see Lonnie in March 1993. He was in hospice care in Newport Beach, and my heart broke to see him so emaciated and in pain. We knocked on the door and were met by his caretaker, who guided us up some stairs to a large room, where Lonnie sat perched on a couch. Though he was a skeleton with skin, he grinned and greeted us warmly. He talked with gusto, telling us how he would be miraculously healed and would continue his preaching ministry around the world.

Laurie reports that Lonnie was sad about the course his life had taken and that he regretted some choices he'd made.

The sun set and Lonnie's caregiver lit a fire in the fireplace. Lonnie kept talking, his face lit by the warm flames. The sight took me back to camps we'd held in the mountains more than 20 years earlier. We'd build a big fire, and Lonnie would preach to all the "Jesus people" while the flames danced and the logs crackled. We were so proud and thankful that he was our preacher.

But it was different now.

The fire was so small, and Lonnie seemed smaller too, like a little boy. His life was flickering out. Mike and I hugged him, told him we loved him, and then we prayed together.

I never saw him again.

If I was writing my life story the way I'd want it, there would be a squeaky-clean version of my conversion. I'd be led to Christ at Billy Graham's knee. No odd puzzle pieces, no ragged edges. No controversy about Lonnie Frisbee, who 30 years later would die of AIDS.

But God used Lonnie powerfully at one time in my life; and in the end I told him so. He is part of my story. God often works through ways that surprise me, ways that I'd never choose. All I know is that He is God, and I am not. (Laurie and Vaughn 138–139)

Bittersweet words. But others express the bitter without the sweet.

"Turns out he was a special kind of sinner," remarks Matt Coker about Lonnie's detractors. "Christians could overlook his past drug use," but not homosexuality. David Di Sabatino comments, "It's like John the Baptist walked through Southern California, and nobody wants to talk about him because he died of AIDS" (Coker, First Jesus Freak).

> Frisbee sported a preacher's collar in the later years. He still had the power to draw crowds, but his sermons had turned bitter. "I need to tell you I moved in big circles," he told one audience, "with big Bozos."

> Bitterness they could take. But when AIDS was cited as the cause of Frisbee's death in 1993, these men of God turned on the machinery of hate. **There were too many witnesses, too many preachers around the world who'd credited Frisbee with setting them on their ministerial paths to simply discount his gift.** Stories spread that he'd hypnotized people all along. He was trashed in a 1997 book titled *Counterfeit Revival*. Evangelicals knew better than anyone how easily the public would accept Frisbee as just another disgraced preacher. It even gave birth to a new philosophy that deemed any "sexual problem" like Frisbee's as the worst sin of all, worse even than murder. (Coker, First Jesus Freak, emphasis mine)

God calls sinners

Author and talk-radio personality the late Rich Buhler asks, "[What does it mean that God] placed His Spirit on a homosexual in 1967? The same thing that it means when God placed His Spirit on any of us who turned our faces up to Him and said, 'Oh, God, please use us! With all our heart we cry out to use us!' Because there aren't any of us who have been used who do not wrestle with sinful issues in our lives" (Di Sabatino).

Obviously God loved Lonnie very much and anointed him greatly—more than any other in his day—to lead many to Christ by a powerful ministry in the Holy Spirit. If God so used Lonnie Frisbee, then those who rejected Lonnie must realize that God has condescended just as deeply to use them. "For all have sinned and fall short of the glory of God" (Rom. 3:23 NIV), and, "There is no one righteous, not even one" (Rom. 3:10 NIV).

In an interview with Matt Coker, Connie Bremer-Murray recalls the early days of her marriage to Lonnie and their ministry.

> People would come from all over the world to sit in our living room and talk to us like we were some kind of gurus. Lonnie and I would look at each other and break out giggling. They would come all this way to hear us say love is the door you open to reach God. But how about feeding them? How about loving them? Churches lock their doors. **My heart goes out to gay people.** Lonnie would say he got saved from that, but… that's no more of a sin than making the children of God live on the lowest rungs. (Coker, Ears on Their Head, emphasis mine)

Smith's Samson controversy

Chuck Smith was the final speaker at Lonnie's memorial service at the Crystal Cathedral in Garden Grove, California. He concluded with comments that Lonnie, like Samson, had not lived up to his full potential.

This angered Connie, who felt such a statement was arrogant and "misunderstood Lonnie completely" (Di Sabatino). But what else would one expect from someone who has been criticized "for drawing connections between disasters (e.g., earthquakes, the September 11 attacks) and divine wrath against homosexuality and abortion"? (Calvary Chapel) Smith had preached all these things.

Lonnie's first mentor in the Haight-Ashbury, Ted Wise, said of Smith's comparing Lonnie to Samson:

> It struck me as so odd, because here's a kid who had nothing by way of education or abilities to even educate himself. What he did with what he had, which is what we're accountable for, I don't know if Chuck has the wherewithal, the place, to say what Lonnie's potential is. If you put it in terms of "What did you do with what you got," Lonnie didn't get much and much wasn't required of him, but *man*, he did a lot with what he had. (Di Sabatino)

"An anointed person is recognized by the power and presence of God upon their life," Di Sabatino says. David Owen, the South African pastor, remarks, "There is a religious body of people that are mad at the fact that God's blessing rested on Lonnie when they think it shouldn't have. And if they had had their choice, Lonnie would not have had the blessing that he did. But he did" (Di Sabatino).

Lonnie's obituary

The *Los Angeles Times* published Lonnie's obituary on March 18, 1993:

> In a ceremony attended by several hundred mourners, Pentecostal minister Lonnie Frisbee, known widely as a "hippie preacher," was laid to rest Wednesday at Crystal Cathedral.
>
> Frisbee, 43, who had a key role in attracting youth to Calvary Chapel of Costa Mesa in the late 1960s and early 1970s, died Friday at his home in Newport Beach after a lengthy illness. Relatives said he died of a brain tumor. …
>
> Lonnie Frisbee was born in Santa Ana and began his preaching career in San Francisco's Haight-Ashbury district when he was only 16, according to family members. …
>
> During funeral services Wednesday morning in Crystal Cathedral, several speakers referred to Frisbee as a preacher who marched to a different drummer. **They said Frisbee's unorthodox ways enabled him to reach out to many who otherwise would not have been receptive to Christian preaching.** (Billiter, emphasis mine)

Lonnie Frisbee: saint or sinner?

Saint or sinner, evangelist or degenerate? Decades after his death, people are still choosing sides.

When documentarian David Di Sabatino approached her about the *Frisbee* film project, Connie Bremer-Murray was eager to help him spread the word about Lonnie. Others weren't so enthusiastic. Says Coker,

One pastor has accused the filmmaker of glorifying homo-sexuality, while another is spreading rumors that Di Sabatino is gay. ("I am not gay," he informs. "I wish I dressed that well, though.") **He finds it ironic that so-called Christians are giving him the same type of un-Christian business they heaped on Frisbee**. "People seem to forget that the underly-ing biblical message is that we're all bastards," Di Sabatino says, "but God loves us anyway." (Coker, First Jesus Freak, emphasis mine)

"I think when we go to heaven, Lonnie won't be the one who was held to account," says Owen. "We are going to be held to account for the way we treated a brother" (Di Sabatino).

Who was this gay hippie preacher, and whatever became of him? He left the mission field too soon. "Lonnie Frisbee is what happens when someone says yes to God and means it" (Lonnie Frisbee: As Were Some).

Lonnie Ray Frisbee was accepted in the Beloved, and he made the most of what God gave him. "God uses anybody who steps up to the table," Di Sabatino points out, "and Lonnie was a man open to God working through him. That's why he's a hero" (Coker, First Jesus Freak). And that's why I love him so.

28. My Testimony

Lonnie Frisbee is a hero to me because my life is similar to his. Unlike Lonnie, I was raised in a Christian home, the son of an evangelical pastor. My parents and our conservative church considered homosexuality a sin. Like Lonnie, throughout my youth I struggled with being gay. I also struggled with my faith because I expected it to deliver me from same-sex attraction.

I strayed from God during high school and college but after a few wild years came to faith and was born again at age twenty-four, when I committed my life to God, Christian morality, and service.

Not wanting to spend my life alone, I met and married a wonderful young woman (one of the youth leaders at my parents' church) and started a Christian house church and a publishing company. I earned a master's degree in biblical studies.

But after eighteen years and many experiences—some good, some disappointing—I realized I could no longer deny who I was simply because the spiritual community I was part of held narrowly prescribed notions of what was acceptable, moral, and holy.

Ex-gay therapy fails

For three decades I had tried everything to rid myself of same-sex desire, including prayer and fasting, deliverance ministry, inner healing, Christian counseling, and finally reparative therapy—the most damaging "treatment" for anyone with same-sex orientation. "Ex-gay" therapy offers nothing but false hope and despair to those struggling to come to terms with accepting themselves and being loved by God.

Gay Christian activist Justin Lee says he could share "hundreds of stories of people who poured their hearts into ex-gay programs, prayer, and other types of therapy, only to discover that neither they nor the others in their programs ever became straight" (Lee 234).

I was one of them, experiencing what nearly everyone does who submits to such treatment: "[Y]ears upon years of trying to change and being told it would happen didn't do anything to make them straight. Instead, it only damaged their faith and their feelings of self-worth" (86).

Rev. Samuel Kader laments that these beleaguered believers

> have been to Christian counselors, they have had hands laid on them in prayer, they have fasted, and begged God to remove the desire in their heart. They have suffered abuse, mistreatment, and when all else failed, they have been ostracized, removed from membership, shunned, and even physically thrown out of church and told never to return. Had there been a way to change their orientation they would have done so. With their prayer to change unanswered, I know personally of gay Christians who have taken their lives because they could no longer bear the pressures to conform. (Kader 2–3)

Lee confirms Kader's findings with his own long-term observations:

As [participants] begin to recognize that their orientation is not changing, they often sink into deep depression, realizing they've wasted years of their lives working for something that was a lie. For people who already started off feeling ostracized and disordered, this can be an absolutely crushing blow. Many blame themselves, beating themselves up for not having enough faith, and in some cases even becoming suicidal. Others blame God or the church; I've lost track of the number of people I've seen lose their faith entirely as a result of their experiences in ex-gay groups. ... **In spite of their public claims, ex-gay ministries are often much more effective at taking away faith than at taking away attractions.** (Lee 236, emphasis mine)

This was precisely my experience. I didn't know then what Alan Chambers, president of Exodus International, a former ex-gay ministry, acknowledged in 2012: 99.9% of those he worked with had experienced *no change* in their orientation.[14] No wonder Exodus closed down in 2013.[15] So have these other reparative ministries:

- In 2012, Love in Action closed, whose executive director of twenty-two years, John Smid, said he had "never met a man who experienced a change from homosexual to heterosexual."[16]

---

14 http://www.patheos.com/blogs/warrenthrockmorton/2012/01/09/alan-chambers-99-9-have-not-experienced-a-change-in-their-orientation/

15 YouTube: Watch Alan Chambers handle questions and comments from ex-gay survivors in "A Room of Ex-Gay Survivors Reacts to Alan Chambers' Apology" at https://www.youtube.com/watch?v=x0SZC3Azsqw.

16 (Baldock, *Walking the Bridgeless Canyon* 298).

- Living Waters Australia shut down permanently in 2014.[17]

- Courage UK changed from trying to "fix" gays to becoming gay-affirming because its leader, Jeremy Marks, after fifteen years in ministry, "announced that *he had never seen one client*, including himself, change sexual orientation."[18]

Michael Johnston is the founder of Americans for Truth, Kerusso Ministries (another now-defunct ex-gay organization), and "National Coming Out of Homosexuality Day."

Johnston was "the darling of anti-gay religious powerhouses. He was awarded by the Southern Baptists and helped write the Assemblies of God's position paper on homosexuality." He also participated in "anti-gay campaigns attempting to use sexual orientation as a criterion to deny fellow citizens equal treatment under the law" (Kincaid).

In 2003, Johnston's Kerusso Ministries disappeared, as did references to him at the American Family Association and Family Policy Network—virulently anti-gay fundamentalist Christian organizations. What happened?

Timothy Kincaid of *Ex-Gay Watch* reveals that "Johnston had been going by the name Sean and had been cruising men online. More surprising, he had been organizing unsafe sex parties and lying about his HIV status" (Kincaid). As reported in *Newsweek*, Johnston "was found to have infected men he'd

---

17 (301).

18 (300).

met online with HIV through unprotected sex" (Schlanger and Wolfson).

Sadly, such stories are common among ex-gay ministries.[19]

The American Psychological Association published a 130-page study in 2009 reporting the harm done to those who have undergone reparative therapy (Baldock, Walking the Bridgeless Canyon 303).

Says researcher Matthew Vines, "The overwhelming majority of gay men and lesbians report that their sexual orientation is both fixed and unchosen" (Vines 28). "Sexual attraction does not go away with prayer and fasting" states Kader. "That is a person's innate orientation. It can be sublimated, it can be denied, but it cannot be driven out" (Kader 5).

Downward spiral

In the winter of 2003, I was diagnosed with testicular cancer. Following surgery came seventeen radiation treatments that ended our hope of having children. (We had lost our only pregnancy a few years previously.)

During that black time, I became disillusioned with the American gospel dream. Marriage and family life weren't working out. The ministry failed to flourish despite the wonderful people who supported us. We suffered from health challenges. Despite my best efforts and beseeching God to deliver me, same-sex desire was still a constant torment.

---

19 See "Desert Scream: Exodus Leader's Shocking Admissions of Ministry's Sexual Abuse" by Wayne Besen at *Truth Wins Out*. https://www.truthwinsout.org/pressrelease/2010/03/7561/.

I paid hundreds of dollars to go through the Living Waters Desert Stream program. It was my last-ditch effort to become straight—acceptable, I thought, to God and the church.

After months of meetings, not only had I not changed, but I no longer had any *hope* for change. Afraid that I would succumb to temptation (I never did), fearing I would shame the Lord, my wife, myself, and discredit the ministry, which might damage the members of our house church, I fell into a deep depression and became mired in suicidal thoughts. I concluded that the only way to escape this nightmare was to end my life.

At my lowest point, I realized I couldn't fix myself and that God wasn't fixing me either—any more than God fixes left-handed people to make them right-handed. I instead needed to be honest, accept who I was, and live my life with integrity, even if it meant losing everything I had built up until then. So I did.

I come out

I dreaded losing my family and being rejected by my friends, but with the support and encouragement of my wife I made the hard decision to come out as a gay man. As a result, we disbanded the ministry and publishing company, divorced amicably, and started over again.

My transition wasn't as quick and painless as I hoped it would be. I was a pastor's son raised in a strict religious environment, married to a woman for eighteen years, politically conservative, and involved in Pentecostal/charismatic Christian ministry. Thankfully, my family stood by me during my transition, but I lost all my church friends. My new "chosen lifestyle" was unacceptable to them. I walked away.[20]

Spirit-filled lesbian minister Elaine Sundby in *Calling the Rainbow Nation Home* states, "[W]e have a Church telling everyone that homosexuals have no place in God's kingdom, and that somehow the 'good news' doesn't include [them]" (Sundby 71). That's what I came to believe, and it was devastating.

I suffered a rough few years trying to find where I belonged. Tired of condemnation from conservative Christianity, I gave up on God. I lost touch with all my former Christian contacts. I struggled to fit in to the gay community, where Christianity is understandably rejected because of the judgment, hate, and persecution many have experienced from the church. Where did I belong?

Bottom of the barrel

I started drinking a lot. Believing that both the church and the Bible condemned me, I turned to alternative spirituality. I lost my self-confidence and, despite the anti-depressants I was taking, again became depressed to the point of suicide.

Gay Pentecostal minister Troy Perry explains what it's like for so many of us:

> We who committed ourselves to a homosexual existence grew gradually to accept a feeling that God did not care about us. That feeling served to place our real spiritual needs under a powerful and almost lethal anesthetic. It took a violent

---

20 I tell the full story in *Response to a Concerned Heterosexual Christian* (Acceptable Books, 2012).

shock as powerful as a bolt of lightning to reveal to me this disgraceful condition arising from our own sense of solitude. (Perry 3)

When things were about as dark as they could be, I had a profound experience.

Looking up, I see light

In the autumn of 2007, the Holy Spirit entered my life in a new way. For weeks I entertained tears and ecstasy, sometimes unable to stand because of waves of power that swept over me. I began receiving new direction, and some signs occurred that were nothing less than astounding. I heard a new voice calling in the desert. Like Perry, "I came through my own personal wilderness, to the oasis in God's garden where I have begun to make my own vision a reality" (7).

God started teaching me about grace and inclusion for all his Kingdom people. The Lord called me to bring Spirit-filled revival to the LGBTQI (lesbian, gay, bisexual, transgender, queer, and intersexed) community.

If God can use Lonnie Frisbee to bring revival to the hippies, God can use me and others to bring revival to the LGBTQI community.

I prayed as Troy Perry prayed, "All right, God, if it's Your will, if You want to see a church started as an outreach into our community, You just let me know when."

I do not yet know how God wants me to fulfill this calling, but I'm open. I started by writing this book.

An impossible choice

In discussing this experience with my ex-wife (we're still good friends), she had some profound things to say, and I heard the voice of the Lord through her words.

Linda C. Howard, MEd, is an administrator at the University of Pittsburgh, a believer who wrote to me in a personal email the following thoughts:

> God does not want to see one person perish. If being gay was such a sin he would take away the desire during the salvation and redemption process. We know this does not happen. Many of our old desires do fall away the closer we get to Jesus, but no matter how much we try to make gayness disappear, it only gets buried. We have to hide who we are because we love God and want to know him more, but the community of God says it's impossible to love God and be gay— which is interesting since God loves us and knows everything about us. Who are we really hiding from? We try to hide who we are until one day it either comes billowing out in nasty ways or we are so lost in the lie we have lived we become depressed, angry, and even self-destructive.
>
> **The truth is, many who were saved at a young age have had to choose between Jesus and who they are—not because of God, but because of the church. And those whom God called later are forced to pretend to be something they aren't in order to fit in to the Christian mold.** Gays are dying and going to hell not because they are gay but because the people of God are afraid, backward, closed-minded, uncaring, and unloving.

It only takes a short study of the Bible to prove the kinds of things God really cares about in his people. He wants us to love and care for others, the sick, the hurting, the lonely, the frightened... If Christians believe homosexuality is truly a sin, the church should put away their club of "religious trans-formation" and practice what Jesus really preached—love, no matter what. If Christians really took the time to know folks who are gay, they would see a community not lost because of sin but because they have been excluded from fellowship.

Yet many Christians still grapple with the apparent differ-ence between what they think the Bible says and what accep-tance of gays in the church may mean.

When souls are at stake, believers with integrity should be willing to re-examine what the Word of God teaches and the love of Christ requires, even if they think they already know all the answers (Acts 17:11). If you're one of these conscientious believers, I'd like to recommend some helpful resources.

Resources for understanding gender, orientation, and Christian faith

Dr. Martyn Lloyd-Jones lays down a "fundamental proposi-tion" for Bible-believing Christians: "[E]verything must be tested by the teaching of Scripture. We must not start with what we think, [or] what we like" (Lloyd-Jones 20). This means we must examine Scripture carefully on any matter before form-ing an opinion. For if we have already formed an opinion—whether that view is based on what we feel is right or, worse, on a misunderstanding or misinterpretation of Scripture—we will, as Jesus indicted the scribes and Pharisees for, make "the Word of God of no effect" (Mark 7:13 NKJV).

It's crucial to be *accurately*, scripturally informed, because if one doesn't fully understand what one is talking about, continuing to quote Scriptures in a non-affirming way amounts to "badgering the… GLBT community with the Bible, the very book that was designed to bring freedom" (Kader 1).

Every Old and New Testament passage concerning same-sex behavior is dealt with carefully and in depth in the following books:

- New Testament professor James V. Brownson applies academic scholarship and moral logic to identify the shortcomings of both traditional and revisionist positions on the Bible and homosexuality in *Bible, Gender, Sexuality: Reframing the Church's Debate on Same-Sex Relationships* (William B. Eerdmans Publishing Co., 2013). Brownson asks Christians to reconsider whether the biblical strictures against same-sex relations as defined in the ancient world should apply to contemporary, committed same-sex relationships.

- *God and the Gay Christian: The Biblical Case in Support of Same-Sex Relationships* by Matthew Vines (Convergent Books, 2014) explores what the Bible does and doesn't say about same-sex relationships and what it means to be a faithful gay Christian.

- In *Openly Gay, Openly Christian* (SEGR Publishing LLC, 2013), Rev. Samuel Kader shares the lessons he has learned from Scripture, history and experience about how the Bible is actually gay-friendly and affirming.

- *Torn: Rescuing the Gospel from the Gays-vs.-Christians Debate* (Jericho Books, 2012) by Justin Lee offers an incisive analysis as well as a solution to the American religious culture war, demonstrating that people of faith on both sides of the debate can respect, learn from, and love one another. He provides practical guidance for all committed Christians who wonder how to relate to gay friends or family members—or who struggle with their own sexuality.

- My own book, *The Sin of Sodom: What the Bible Really Teaches About Why God Destroyed the Cities of the Plain* (Acceptable Books, 2015) reveals what the sins of Sodom and Gomorrah were, detailing every mention in the Bible and reviewing the theological development of church opinion about the subject.

- Kathy Baldock provides a history of homosexuality in American society, looks at religion and politics, and examines how the church can make things better for the LGBT community in her excellent and comprehensive volume *Walking the Bridgeless Canyon: Repairing the Breach Between the Church and the LGBT Community* (Canyonwalker Press, 2014).

For a complete list of helps, see "Appendix: Recommended Resources" on page 199.

29. Awaking to the Call

As mentioned previously, the Holy Spirit entered my life in a powerful way in October 2007, when God began speaking to me about what he was calling me to do. I wrote down the following prophetic words then and share them here for the first time.

The new fold and the awakening

Concerned that I had failed God and forsaken his original call on my life because of my inability to overcome homosexuality, he reassured me:

> I have not forsaken you, but I have made adjustments. I now desire you to go forth with renewed faith and confidence that I am using you to reach the lost, those who need my love and guidance. **I have many sheep, my son. They are not of the fold you have been part of.** I have called you to leave the ninety-nine and find the one. But there are many—*many* I say—who are lost and are rejected by the [under]shepherd and the ninety-nine. Go to them and bring them unto my bosom, the heart of the Great Shepherd, and I will reward you and provide all that you need for the work. (2007/10/21)

I felt at the time this had to do with reaching the gay community. The following day, the Lord again spoke to me about *beginning a new move of the Spirit.* I asked him what he was about to birth.

> **I am about to bring about an awakening.** I am about to open the eyes of those born blind. I am about to open the ears of the deaf in every area and arena of life, and I am about to show myself strong on behalf of my kingdom. I want my kingdom to be established, not the kingdoms of men and of religion. I desire people with hearts aflame, and not dead institutions where people become locked and stagnant, as if in a prison. I desire to open minds and free spirits that they might do the work that I have ordained from the foundation of the world.

> **I have many sheep you know not of. I have those I desire to bring into the fold. But it is not a fold of man's making, designed to keep others out. I will remake the fold, and I will establish new boundaries. My fold is all-inclusive, and there will be no time or place for bickering and disagreement over doctrine and practices.** (2007/10/22)

I knew this new fold would include LGBTQI[21] believers. God says in Isaiah 56:8, "Yet will I *gather others* to him, *beside those* that are gathered unto him" (KJV). Jesus said, "I have *other sheep* that are not of this sheep pen. I must bring them also. *They too will listen to my voice,* and there shall be *one flock* and *one shepherd*" (John 10:16 NIV).

---

21 Lesbian, gay, bisexual, transgender, queer, intersexed. For an explanation of terms, see http://geneq.berkeley.edu/lgbt_resources_definiton_of_terms and http://www.christianitytoday.com/ct/2015/july-august/understanding-transgender-gender-dysphoria.html.

God's "new move"

God's word to me was confirmed by the following account in Rev. Elaine Sundby's *Calling the Rainbow Nation Home.*

In the early 1990s, Washington state pastors Evelyn and Dennis Schave sought God with fasting and prayer for their church. They were impressed that the Lord had "something bigger" in mind for them. God impressed upon them that "they were not to judge anyone that came through their church doors" (Sundby 141).

More and more gay couples began to attend their church in the coming months and, finding they were not condemned, invited their friends. These gays were getting saved and growing in their faith. But they weren't being delivered of homosexuality.

Original (heterosexual) members took issue with the Schaves for not imposing moral standards on the new members. But the Holy Spirit had told the Schaves that he would do any "cleaning up" that was needed.

"If the Holy Spirit wanted these people to stop being homosexuals," says Sundby, "it was his job—not theirs—to make that happen. Reminded of this, Evelyn and Dennis remained true to their vow, and more gay folks continued to swell their ranks" (141–142).

The situation came to the attention of their denomination, resulting in Dennis's removal as the Northwest District Coordinator. This threatened their ministry and their approaching retirement.

About this time, Evelyn received an invitation to minister at an Advance conference (now The Alliance), an organization that supports and encourages churches that openly accept LGBT people. Evelyn felt conflicted but kept her promise to minister.

As soon as she arrived at the conference, she encountered powerful worship among the gay and lesbian believers there, and she was overcome by the power of the Holy Spirit. "God's holiness and the gifts of the Spirit were very strong that night," she says (147).

The presence of God was so thick, in tears she phoned her husband, held up the receiver so that he could hear the worship, and he also broke down, for they both knew: "This *was* the 'new thing' from God they had been waiting for and *these* were the people they were supposed to minister to" (147).

God will pour out the Holy Spirit on the LGBTQI community

When I read these words in May 2015, the Holy Spirit fell on me, and I began to shake and weep. Beyond the shadow of a doubt, I *knew* this awakening, this *"new move"* God had told me about on October 22, 2007, was an outpouring of the Spirit upon the LGBTQI community, and I had a part to play in it. The Lord then told me why:

> I desire to pour my Spirit out upon the world, and I will do this that I might accomplish in these final days all that I have set in my heart to do. **It will begin with a birth, an awakening, and the baby will be spirited away for a time, that it might be raised in seclusion and safety.**

I believe this "spiriting away for a time" refers to the pioneering work of men like the Rev. Troy Perry, founder of Metropolitan Community Churches[22]; Mel White of Soulforce[23];

and of course Lonnie Frisbee, the prototype of Spirit-empow-
ered revival among the disenfranchised. Since their work in
the early days, a tremendous backlash developed in the conservative church against the gay community, driving the gay
church into seclusion for a time.

Like the infant Moses, whom God hid until the time of his
release to deliver God's people from bondage, like the baby
Jesus, whom God spirited away to Egypt until those who
threatened his development were deposed, although the work
of the Spirit among gay Christians has been nurtured in the
background for an entire generation, the Lord has not stopped
working his plan. The gay church is returning to take center
stage in God's strategy for worldwide deliverance and salvation.

The Lord continued to speak to me:

The enemy desires to thwart what I have destined to come
into the earth, but he shall not have his way. **I will birth my
child and shall hide it in the bosom of the forgotten until it
is weaned. Then I will bring about the changes that will
amaze and confound the shepherds of the fold until none
who love me can gainsay it.** I desire to use you to help raise
my child and to minister to the forgotten that they might be
equipped to raise my child for its entrance into the world.

When I first learned about Lonnie Frisbee in March 2015, I
ordered David Di Sabatino's documentary, *Frisbee: The Life
and Death of a Hippie Preacher* (2006). The Holy Spirit moved

---

22 http://mccchurch.org/

23 http://www.soulforce.org/

on me as it played, and through my tears God began to deal with and speak to me.

I experienced the same touching presence when I viewed *Call Me Troy* (2007), a documentary about the life and ministry of gay Christian pioneer Rev. Troy Perry.

Watching these DVDs and reading about Lonnie renewed my call. Although I did not know back in 2007 what the Spirit of God meant when he spoke about a "new move" and an "all-inclusive fold," I since have received clarifying messages.

> For surely I have called you… to go forth into the wilderness and to preach the gospel to those that are not accepted in the general fold. **But they are accepted in the Beloved, and they are included in the Body, and I desire that you go to them and that you prepare them, that they might receive my blessing and the outpouring of the Spirit, that they might be prepared for the coming Kingdom.** For I desire to use them also to reach those round about them and to draw them all into the fold that the Great Shepherd is making. (2015/04/23)

The following day, the Spirit spoke to me this message of assurance:

> I am calling you forth to go unto the lost, to find those who do not know which way to turn, who do not know whom to connect with or where to go to satisfy the longing of their heart. **I desire that you bring the message of acceptance to them and that you give them that word which will encourage them and let them know that they are included and they are beloved of the Father.**

For there is not one who cannot be reached. There is not one which does not belong. There is not one who has no place at the table in your Father's Kingdom. For there are seats for everyone, and I desire that they all be filled.

I desire that you go out and extend the invitation to the banqueting table: there is a feast that has been made ready, and there is much rejoicing and celebration to enjoy. For this Kingdom feast is not a solemn occasion, but it is an occasion of joy and rejoicing, of upliftment and encouragement. (2015/04/24)

Building the bridge

Mainstream churches have grown more inclusive and affirming to LGBT believers for some years now. But conservative churches—especially charismatic and Pentecostal denominations and independent fellowships—lag behind. I want to build a bridge to the Spirit-baptized churches, educating about the true meaning of inclusion in the Scriptures.

My heart's desire is to be used of God to evangelize the LGBTQI community, bringing Pentecostal revival to those outside the greater fold, leaving the ninety-nine (the traditional church) to find the lost and bring them back to the heart of the Great Shepherd. As Lonnie did, I want to preach the gospel of the Kingdom in Jesus' name with signs, wonders, and miracles to confirm the Word in the power of the Holy Spirit.

I also want to spark repentance and renewal in churches open to affirming and reconciling with their gay spiritual siblings. For, as Rev. Samuel Kader proclaims, "The church is not called to be the judge of the world. ... God has given to the church the ministry of reconciliation, not the ministry of alienation" (Kader 10–11).

Accepted in the Beloved

On October 31, 2007, the Lord revealed a few things that would bring me to the place of my commissioning. They all have to do with the concept of acceptance.

- You are "accepted in the Beloved" (Ephesians 1:6).
- You will be accepted as a gay man among your friends, associates, and faith community.
- You will receive the acceptance of your parents, conservative evangelicals.
- Your spiritual gifts to reach the lost will be accepted.
- Every tribe, tongue, and nation will stand before the throne of God, including the LGBTQI community.

The Holy Spirit then spoke this word to me:

> I am calling you to a ministry of acceptance, my son. First, you must accept what I show you. Then you must accept your part to play in that which I'm calling you to do. Then you must accept those to whom I send you, that you might minister to them in the Spirit, who will help them to accept what I am saying. Accept my call on your life, and I will make you acceptable to those I call you to. (2007/10/31)

In *Openly Gay, Openly Christian*, Kader relates the testimony of Steve Parker, a young gay Christian. After being rejected by the church and nearly ruining his life with drugs and alcohol, Steve accepted himself as gay and found that God was still there for him, had never stopped loving him. It was only at this point of acceptance that he began to experience God's presence again. "Because I came to accept myself and love myself as I was, homosexuality and all," says Steve, "I could now accept God's love for me" (5–7).

Beyond loving God with your whole being, Jesus calls us to "Love your neighbor *as yourself*" (Matt. 22:39). The Lord has ministered healing to me, restored me, and drawn me back to himself. As I write this now, signs and wonders are occurring to bring these prophecies to pass. Finally, I have accepted myself, accepted others, and accepted that God can use even me.

30. Can God Use Gays?

In Di Sabatino's documentary, author and talk-radio personality the late Rich Buhler says, "I think Lonnie was a very authentic person. He was an authentic man of God who had a childlike freedom to be used of God, and when he was doing it, he was being authentic."

But Buhler also felt Lonnie "was an authentic screwed-up person with some very deep, deep pain that he didn't even know the significance of" (Di Sabatino). Some believed this maladjustment stemmed from Lonnie's sexual abuse at an early age. One problem with Di Sabatino's documentary is it seems to presuppose that sexual abuse is the cause of homosexuality.

Does sexual abuse cause homosexuality?

Richard B. Gartner, PhD, faculty member and founding director of the Sexual Abuse Program at the William Alanson White Institute reports, "Conventional wisdom says sexual abuse turns boys gay, although there's no persuasive evidence that premature sexual activity fundamentally changes sexual orientation" (Gartner).

The American Psychiatric Association states in its online fact sheet, "LGBT Sexual Orientation":

[N]o specific psychosocial or family dynamic cause for homosexuality has been identified, including histories of

159

childhood sexual abuse. Sexual abuse does not appear to be more prevalent in children who grow up to identify as gay, lesbian, or bisexual, than in children who identify as heterosexual (American Psychiatric Association).

Childhood or adolescent abuse may cause serious problems, but it does not automatically make one homosexual, nor does healing abuse change one's sexual orientation. There are plenty of people who were *not* sexually abused or rejected by their fathers, yet they are still gay.

"[T]here is nothing to indicate that parenting or early-childhood events, such as abuse, affect either gender or sexual orientation," according to Baldock (Baldock, Walking the Bridgeless Canyon 214).

Being gay is not a sickness or maladjustment that needs to be healed. It is a natural orientation that must be accepted. If more gays and lesbians were viewed this way, the more well-adjusted they would be.

How important are sex, gender, and orientation?

The Apostle Paul prophesied about the future progression of the church: "There is neither Jew nor Gentile, neither slave nor free, *nor is there male and female,* for you are all one in Christ Jesus" (Gal. 3:28 NIV).

The early church, which began with Jewish believers, had trouble incorporating the Gentiles. The American church in the nineteenth century argued over the abolition of slavery. Women's rights and equality took the stage in the twentieth century. And in the twenty-first century, gender and orientation issues are challenging traditional ideas of morality and faith. In a *Christianity Today* article, Andy Crouch explains,

What unites the LGBTQIA coalition is a conviction that human beings are not created male and female in any essential or important way. What matters is not one's body but one's heart—the seat of human will and desire, which only its owner can know. ... [E]mbodied sexual differentiation is irrelevant—completely, thoroughly, totally irrelevant—to covenant faithfulness. ... To insist on the importance of bodies is to challenge the sovereign self, to suggest that our ethical options are limited by something we did not choose. (Crouch)

Physical sex, like gender (social roles based on the sex of the person, usually culturally learned[24]), are not determiners of acceptability to God or inclusion in Christ. Neither is a person's sexual orientation—"an enduring pattern of romantic or sexual attraction (or a combination of these) to persons of the opposite sex or gender, the same sex or gender, or to both sexes or more than one gender" (Sexual orientation). God spoke to the prophet Samuel and said, "Humans only care about the external appearance, but the Eternal considers the inner character" (1 Sam. 16:7 VOICE).

Most of the church has a long way to go. The inkling of acceptance seen today did not exist in the 1960s, 70s, 80s, and 90s. Lonnie's being rejected by both his biological father and step-father, then by his spiritual fathers Chuck Smith and John Wimber, no doubt took its toll on his emotional health. Lonnie became understandably bitter about this rejection.

---

24 https://en.wikipedia.org/wiki/Sex_and_gender_distinction

God's love experienced through self-acceptance

Whether these men or Lonnie himself felt being gay was a sickness or sin doesn't make it so. It just made Lonnie—and millions of other LGBT people—feel bad about themselves.

Commenting on her experience of coming out as both gay and Christian, Elaine Sundby understands that "my bondage had never been the 'sin' of homosexuality, but instead my guilt and despair over *belief* that it was a sin" (Sundby 90). Troy Perry speaks of being haunted by an "awful conviction that if you were a homosexual you could not be a child of God; you could not be a Christian" (Perry 132). Sundby remarks, "With so many people telling me I was going to hell, I couldn't help but wonder if I really was saved" (Sundby 63).

Kader declares, "Countless lives are being battered, bruised, and damaged, by maintaining this tradition" that homosexuality and Christianity are incompatible, that LGBT people cannot be saved or used of God (Kader 2).

> People who have tried everything the church offered discovered their innate feelings have never gone away. These feelings are as much a part of who they are as feelings in the heterosexual are innate to them. In so many cases the church is not offering help and hope. Rather, they are offering bondage and legalism, bound to a tradition that has no power to help. (4)

Yet, as one gay professional realized when he finally accepted Christ, "He was there all along but I had kept Him at arm's length because I never felt I was good or worthy enough to be accepted by Him. He took me as I was, and that fact

allowed me to let God love me and I was able to love myself"
(Johnson).

Salvation has nothing to do with one's sexual orientation,
but everything to do with one's acceptance or rejection of Jesus
Christ (Sundby 70).

Lonnie Frisbee: "The most influential gay man in twentieth-century Christianity"

When Di Sabatino learned from Connie Bremer-Murray that
Lonnie defined himself as being gay, it was "a game changer"
for him. "I had to rethink everything." Di Sabatino points out
that "God had called Lonnie *while* he was gay. … What did it
mean that God had chosen a homosexual to be his representa-
tive?" (Exclusive Interview)

Did God not know who Lonnie was at his core? Did God
not know what he was doing in calling this young man?

Kathy Baldock reminds us, "The revival began with the
most unlikely of people—a gay hippie who many said looked
like Jesus Himself. **God anointed and called Lonnie Frisbee
to birth a Holy Spirit movement within the hippie counterculture**" (Baldock, Walking the Bridgeless Canyon 356, emphasis mine).

Blogger Anita Mathias indicates, "Of all the people [God]
could have chosen to unleash the wave of the Spirit which
reached the nations through the Vineyard, he chose a tor-
mented gay person, Lonnie Frisbee."

Mathias considers Lonnie to be "**the most influential gay
man in twentieth-century Christianity**, a key person in the
Jesus People or Jesus Freak movement, who unleashed a wave
of the Holy Spirit which was instrumental in the founding and
phenomenal growth of two major Christian denominations."

Whether hippies or homosexuals, "God sees their hearts, the whole man or woman, and sees someone he can use as his conduit of grace" (Mathias, emphasis mine).

God called a gay man

Di Sabatino remarks, "Even if you believe homosexuality is a sin, I still cannot understand why they single that behavior out as opposed to pride or judgmentalism or obesity." Instead, he assures us all:

> God reaches out to anyone willing to be used, and... **Lonnie's true importance of being called while a homosexual way back in 1967 was to tell a generation of young believers that God was ahead of the curve, inviting those that the contemporary church had excluded.** (Exclusive Interview, emphasis mine)

God manifested the power of the Holy Spirit through Lonnie Frisbee to bring many into the Kingdom. "To admit that would be to admit that God used a gay hippie with a drug history," says Hardin Crowder, "and we seem to prefer the idea that God only uses 'good people' to do his work" (Crowder).

Lonnie's ex-wife Connie Bremer-Murray says, "Lonnie never saw himself as being special. He saw that **everybody could have what he had**, and he actually promoted people" (Coker, Ears on Their Head, emphasis mine).

But those who benefited from his anointing—personally and in the explosive growth of their own ministries—have pitied him, written him off, or even denounced him *and* the ministries that grew from his influence.

Some people, Di Sabatino believes, simply "cannot fathom that God would choose to risk His reputation by aligning Himself with someone of Frisbee's background" (Jackson, *Quest* 388). Di Sabatino takes it a step further:

The shameful tendency of American "cult" and apologetics demagogues to utilize the slur tactics of guilt by association leaves those with Frisbee in their spiritual lineage open to rancorous condemnation. Hank Hanegraaff's *Counterfeit Revival* is the most egregious example of this perplexing style where the author impugns the Vineyard movement as having "structural defects" for even associating with Frisbee. Hanegraaff accuses Wimber of turning "his pulpit over to a… hypnotist struggling with homosexuality."

In his rebuttal to Hanegraaff's book, James A. Beverley writes in *Revival Wars: A Critique of Counterfeit Revival* that **behind the desire to distance Christian history from someone like Frisbee "is the notion that God could not possibly use someone struggling with homosexuality."** Not only does Hanegraaff's logic fail to point the same accusatory finger at Calvary Chapel for having Frisbee in its spiritual lineage, but it fails to recognize the obvious biblical reality that **sinless perfection is not a prerequisite for being used by God.**

As embarrassing as Lonnie Frisbee's story may be to many of those who were influenced by him, the fact remains that **God called him while he was an LSD-ingesting hypnotist who was experimenting with alternative sexuality just as God called Paul as he was a murderer.** To miss the underlying premise of Frisbee's biography—that God would risk His reputation by aligning Himself to such a frail character—is to ignore the potential that lies resonant within each of us. That God "chose the lowly things of this world and the despised things" (1 Cor. 1:28) should cause us to rejoice with humility. (389, emphasis mine)

Where can gays find grace?

Guilt by association... talking trash... blanket condemnation. "Little children with big cruelties," as Lonnie said of his childhood tormentors.

This is what gay people have faced and still face in the church today—even gay believers who have diligently sought to deny their desires and orientation. If they continue to attend non-affirming churches, they are forced to hide who they are.

Gay minister Troy Perry admits that during this phase of his life, "I kept going to church, but I felt so hypocritical about it. It was like going to a Ku Klux Klan meeting but not believing that blacks, Catholics and Jews were inferior" (Perry 105).

Where can gay Christians go for grace? Chuck Smith Jr remarks that early on his father did say before his congregation,

> "If we have to turn away one young person because they're barefoot, and their bare feet are going to ruin our carpet, then we'll pull out the carpet, remove the pews, and we'll sit on the concrete floor. These kids have nowhere else to go to connect with God. If we turn them away, where do they go?" (Di Sabatino)

"Now, we can say that about drug-dealing, free-sex, rock-and-roll hippies," claims Smith Jr, "but *not* say that about homosexuals? If the Church says to anyone, 'You cannot come here, you cannot engage in the life of the Church' to anyone, then where are they supposed to go to find Jesus?'" (Di Sabatino)

At *As Were Some of You*, an anonymous blogger reacts about the eventual acceptance of hippies but the continued rejection of gays.

> The connections between the hippies of the 60s and the homosexuals of the 06s cannot be ignored. The hippies were considered freaks… dirty… anti-American and possessing a disgusting, anti-family lifestyle. The hippies, man, were all about love. Free love, costly love, they wanted to know more. I swear, the more I stand and draw parallels between the hippies and the homosexuals today, the more it makes me shake with anger. **The same thing is happening today. We have not remembered history and we are condemned to repeat it.** (Lonnie Frisbee: As Were Some, emphasis mine)

The church's rejection of LGBTQI folks parades as holiness and righteousness but is far from the heart of God and the love of Christ. Connie Bremer-Murray reveals that after she left Lonnie, for a time even she fell for this religious perversion of Christianity.

> I blocked abortion-clinic doors. It seemed so right. But after the third or fourth time, God jerked me by the collar and said, "Would I do this stuff? Would I do this anywhere?" You need to walk with him to get those messages. The enemy comes as an angel of [light], appearing as good and right. Don't expect the enemy to have horns and steam coming off him. I believe the enemy will come right out of the [midst] of the religious-right movement. (Coker, Ears on Their Head)

Di Sabatino indicates that such behavior does not represent all followers of Christ.

> Some of us are upset that that's who people think of as Christians today. I think people are seduced by the same thing Christians are supposed to rail against: power and money. Those things have nothing to do with Jesus. What's even worse is they use fear as a motivational tool. Fear has nothing to do with faith. What scares me to death is their image of judgment. Some of these people are going to come up, say they did all these things, and God is going to say, "You're not on my team; you didn't get it." (Coker, Ears on Their Head)

Connie continues the conversation:

> When Jesus looks at [these people], he's going to say they have ears attached to their heads, but they don't hear. **When they say gay people are all sinners [who] ought to read this passage of the Bible, they don't get it.** You're supposed to read it as if it's written as a personal letter to you, not for you to impose on everyone else. There are more atrocities done in God's name—more than in Hitler's name. It's what God calls fornicating the truth. And when you mix that with lies, that's called deception. (Coker, Ears on Their Head, emphasis mine)

Sins on a scale?

Which is worse, sexual sin or judgmentalism? To those Christians who prided themselves on leading cleaner lives than the rankest of sinners, Paul wrote:

> Those people are on a dark spiral downward. But if you think that leaves you on the high ground where you can point your finger at others, think again. Every time you criticize

someone, you condemn yourself. It takes one to know one.
Judgmental criticism of others is a well-known way of
escaping detection in your own crimes and misdemeanors.
But God isn't so easily diverted. He sees right through all
such smoke screens and holds you to what you've done.
—*ROMANS 2:1–2 MSG*

We must be careful to discern that sin here is promiscuity
and self-devaluation, not being gay in itself. Elaine Sundby
points out that if homosexuals cannot be saved, "We would
have to believe that Christ did not conquer sin, *but rather that
a single sin conquered him*" (Sundby 69). Troy Perry states: "The
real sins are hate and being inhuman to each other" (Perry vi).
This is what happened to Lonnie Frisbee.

God ordains gay ministers

"Lonnie's misfortune," says Chuck Smith Jr, "is that he got
caught, because there are a lot of charismatic homosexual ministers, right now. ... We need to find a way within the Body of
Christ to love and minister to them and accommodate them"
(Di Sabatino).

Yet Mathias understands that "fruitful ministry (prophecy,
healing, and preaching)... is unavailable to non-celibate gays
in most every Christian denomination" (Mathias). One anonymous person commented on Mathias's article this way:

Perhaps the great turmoil men like Frisbee undergo is
because they are convinced by the evangelical template/
mindset that they need to deny their sexuality. Authentic
homosexuality is not a choice... to therefore deny it is to state
that God made a mistake.... Perhaps, also, it may be helpful
to avoid the stereotypical examples of those who have had

abusive beginnings as reason for particular sexuality. ...
**Lonnie Frisbee birthed two movements.... Perhaps God
was making a statement here?**" (Mathias)

The greatest revival in the twentieth century was catalyzed
by a young gay hippie. Obviously, God knew what he was
doing because millions were saved and believed on the Lord
Jesus Christ through Lonnie's ministry.

What the Holy Spirit demonstrated in prototype through
Lonnie Frisbee is now being replicated in the greater LGBTQI
community. The Church needs these precious people because
God's banquet table is not yet full.[25]

---

25 See Matthew 22:9–10; Luke 14:13–14, 21–23.

31. The Church Needs LGBTQI Believers

Christian social scientist Tony Campolo made an important and historical announcement on June 8, 2015.

Campolo promotes complete inclusion

Campolo stated for the record, "It has taken countless hours of prayer, study, conversation and emotional turmoil to bring me to the place where I am finally ready to call for the full acceptance of Christian gay couples into the Church." This is significant for a devout Bible-believing evangelical.

Through years of experience with gay Christian couples his wife Peggy knows, Campolo concluded that

> sexual orientation is almost never a choice and I have seen how damaging it can be to try to "cure" someone from being gay. As a Christian, my responsibility is not to condemn or reject gay people, but rather to love and embrace them, and to endeavor to draw them into the fellowship of the Church. When we sing the old invitation hymn, "Just As I Am," I want us to mean it, and I want my gay and lesbian brothers and sisters to know it is true for them too. (Campolo)

Acceptance is not enough

In response to Compolo's full acceptance of gay and lesbian Christians, writer Brandan Robertson at *Revangelical* proclaims, "A new day is dawning in Christianity, indeed. The

Spirit of God is moving on the hearts of Christian pastors, leaders, and laypeople alike and causing many to return to the Scriptures again with fresh eyes, listening to the still small voice of the Holy Spirit calling us to see a more expansive and inclusive vision of Christ's Church" (Robertson). Yet, says Robertson,

> It is not enough that Christian leaders simply step forward and announce their support for gay and lesbian Christians. It's also important that they acknowledge the harm that has been caused by their use of an un-affirming theology and that they publicly repent for their sin of exclusion. This is a key move that many Christian leaders who have changed their mind have not considered, but is perhaps even more important than announcing their support for inclusion and equality. In order for LGBTQ [people] to find the healing that we need, the acknowledgment of the oppression and harm we have faced at the hands of Christian pastors, teachers, and theologians is essential. (Robertson)

Inclusion must lead to ministry

The church's repentance, apology, and full acceptance of LGBTQI believers includes more than just allowing them to sit in the pews. It means releasing them into ministry and embracing all their gifts to the Body.

Gays have much to offer that's useful to God and his people. Black gospel music historian Anthony Heilbut asks, "Where would religious art be without gay men? And if we were to get rid of all the gospel hymns written and performed by gays that people have been saved to?" (Harrison)

Exclusion is more serious than loss of talent, however. "By discarding so many LGBT men and women of God," says Baldock, "the Christian church has lost out on the full, rich diversity and spiritual gifts of countless Christians" (Baldock, Walking the Bridgeless Canyon 363). "Many fail to recognize the loss to conservative churches of almost two generations of excellent pastors, leaders, and servants. We have a generation of young gay, lesbian, bisexual, and transgender Christians growing up in our churches now. How shall we treat them?" (372)

Improving the church's track record

The church holds a poor track record of accepting the outcast, at least in recent history, and the world has noticed.

In *unChristian: What a New Generation Really Thinks About Christianity*, David Kinnaman and Gabe Lyons report, "Outsiders say our hostility toward gays—not just opposition to homosexual politics and behaviors but disdain for gay individuals—has become virtually synonymous with the Christian faith" (Kinnaman and Lyons 92).

In *Torn: Rescuing the Gospel from the Gays-vs.-Christians Debate*, Justin Lee concurs. "The church's 'antihomosexual' reputation isn't just a reputation for opposing gay sex or gay marriage; it's a reputation for *hostility to gay people*" (Lee 3).

Pride and shame in Christian ministry

In his day, Lonnie was one of the most well known of the Christian ministers, worship leaders, and musicians who were outed. Others however, chose to come out, refusing to live a lie. Although they had struggled, they overcame and were able to reconcile their faith and sexuality (Lonnie Frisbee – Gay Vessel).

These honest believers include vocalist Ray Boltz, who wrote and performed such contemporary Christian hits as "Watch the Lamb" and "Thank You (for Giving to the Lord)"; singer and songwriter Marsha Stevens, who at sixteen wrote the anthem of the Jesus Movement, "For Those Tears I Died"; recording artist Jennifer Knapp; "King of Gospel Music" James Cleveland; Anthony Williams ("Tonex"); Kirk Talley; Clay Aiken of *American Idol* fame; and megachurch pastor Jim Swilley[26]. Pentecostal minister Troy Perry came out and started his own church and denomination for gay and lesbian Christians, the Universal Fellowship of Metropolitan Community Churches.

Others have been caught and shamed: prophet Roberts Liardon[27], prophet and healing evangelist Paul Cain[28], and pastor Ted Haggard[29]. And what of Lonnie Frisbee?

> **[B]eing gay was not his downfall; rather, [it was] his failure to accept his sexual orientation as God-ordained and a gift from God.** If Frisbee had accepted his sexual orientation earlier, he would not have lived a double life and [could have been] authentic in his relationships. (Lonnie Frisbee – Gay Vessel, emphasis mine)

Lonnie's conflict was between his faith-based beliefs and his innate sexuality. What are the results of this inner conflict in LGBTQI people today?

---

26 (Out of the Closet).

27 (Butcher).

28 (Grady).

29 (Haggard Admits 'Inappropriate Relationship') and (Cooperman).

The results of rejection

Matthew Vines' friend Josh came out only to be rejected by his family and his Bible-believing church. "In time," Vines recounts, "he found it impossible to keep believing in a loving God. As he saw it, the God of the Bible required him to hate a core part of himself. Not surprisingly, he also gave up on the Bible, since it had been the instrument that taught others to reject that part of him too" (Vines 7).

The traditionally unaffirming teaching that developed in the church over the last century has led many LGBTQIs to believe that not only God's people, but God himself, rejects them. And not only rejects them, but hates them.

"[N]o other teaching that Christians widely continue to embrace," says Vines, "has caused anything like the torment, destruction, and alienation from God that the church's rejection of same-sex relationships has caused" (Vines 158). Instead of making gay believers more Christ-like, as turning from actual sin would do, "embracing a non-affirming position makes them less like God" (161–162).

When gays are met with rejection, hostility, or even behavioral qualifications not placed on others, it sends the strong message that they cannot come to God as they are—and that they will never be accepted unless they conform to standards impossible for them to meet. The vast majority have already tried to do so in order to find acceptance and have met with failure and additional rejection.

"By condemning homosexuality," says Vines, "the church was shutting off a primary avenue for relational joy and companionship in gay people's lives" (12). A life without relational connection cannot be fully human (155).

In a survey of transgender Christians, Christian psychologist Mark Yarhouse's research team at the Institute for the Study of Sexual Identity asked, "What kind of support would you have liked from the church?" One person answered, "Someone to cry with me rather than just denounce me. Hey, it is scary to see God not rescue someone from cancer or schizophrenia or [gender dysphoria]... but learn to allow your compassion to overcome your fear and repulsion" (Yarhouse).

Justin Lee, speaking to the Christian community, laments, "Tragically, our treatment of LGBT people is one place where we've failed over and over again, and the neighbors Jesus taught us to love are the ones who have paid the price for our sins as a church" (Lee 226).

Even those who feel they're taking a godly stance by "loving the sinner but hating the sin" don't realize the damage they're doing to LGBTQIs.

> When someone says they're "loving the sinner," it sounds as though the person being referred to is a "sinner" in some sense that the speaker is not. That's not a biblical picture. According to the Bible, all of us are sinners, equally fallen in God's eyes, and all of us have been shown so much grace by God that we have absolutely no right to look down on anyone else (227–228).

Tony Campolo quips, "Jesus never says, 'Love the sinner, but hate his sin.' Jesus says, 'Love the sinner, and hate your *own* sin'" (228).

One young gay man was asked about his faith experience. He replied, "I don't go to church and don't know anything about Christians except that they HATE homosexuals." Says late humorist Barbara Johnson, "What a sad commentary— that we Christians should be known for our dislike or hatred of others, rather than for our love" (Johnson 135). Vines believes that God's image will be sullied until LGBT believers are welcomed unreservedly into the body of Christ (Vines 177).

Excluded from the Kingdom

At Canyonwalker Connections, author of *Walking the Bridgeless Canyon: Repairing the Breach Between the Church and the LGBT Community*, Kathy Baldock knows that out there in the LGBTQI community are those who "do love God, love Jesus and long for the Holy Spirit." But, she says, "When the face of persecution is Christianity, it will be the rare gay, lesbian, bisexual or transgender faith-seeker that will gravitate *towards* the persecutors" (Baldock, Uncomfortable).

Such maltreatment by people who claim to love Christ slams shut the door to the Kingdom of heaven—not only on the gays and lesbians they personally encounter—but *everyone these individuals are connected to.* "How, then, can they call on the one they have not believed in? And how can they believe in the one of whom they have not heard? And how can they hear without someone preaching to them?" (Rom. 10:14 NIV)

When those rejected by the church stand before God, the first question will not be, *Were you a homosexual?* The first question will be, *What did you do with my offer of salvation?* (Johnson 129)

We must understand what is really at stake with the inclusion and full acceptance of LGBTQI believers and what they have to offer the church, the Kingdom, and the world. **The greatest ploy of the enemy is to keep people—as individuals or entire classes—out of ministry to stop the move of the Holy Spirit.**

"No wonder Satan has been so diligent in his war against the gay community," proclaims Kader, "because it is one of the last remnant groups to be accepted by the Body" (Kader 204).

Destruction precedes a delivering move of God

We often see an outpouring of hate and destruction before a great move of God.

Pharaoh commanded the death of all Hebrew male children, which would have prevented Moses from coming on the scene to deliver God's people from bondage (Ex. 1:15–17).

King Herod of Israel ordered the death of all male children under the age of two to prevent the Messiah, the new King of Israel, from coming to power (Matt. 2:16–18).

Under Germany's Third Reich, nearly 15,000 men were forced to wear a pink triangle that identified them as homosexuals. They were typically placed in "special slave-labor squads and were subjected to medical experiments," all of which contributed to their higher mortality rate in Hitler's concentration camps (Heger). Baldock points out that, along with millions of Jews, "an estimated one million German gays were targeted in the Holocaust" (Baldock, Uncomfortable).

The destruction of the Jews in an attempt to wipe out God's chosen people may have prevented the fulfilment of prophecies that precede the first and second comings Christ. But what about the gays?

Could it be that their disenfranchisement and destruction through the efforts of political and religious leaders are a ploy to prevent the final harvest before the close of this age?

What if gays were accepted and embraced by the church? What if they were empowered by the living Christ and anointed with the Holy Spirit to reach those whom only they can reach? To bring grace and love and healing to them so that *they* can be set free to minister the same to others?

It would produce an outpouring of spiritual power the likes of which the world has never seen, eclipsing even the Jesus Movement.

LGBTQIs needed for the Great Commission

The Great Commission is the heart of Christ. Unfortunately, it is not the heart of most Christians or churches.

The greater Body must embrace and support LGBTQI believers and enable them to evangelize.

If LGBTQIs cannot become secure that God and his people accept them completely and their sexuality is no longer an issue, then what's the point in having an "evangelical" church? By continuing to be rejected and marginalized, they'll continue to question how they see themselves and will lack the confidence and faith to take the good news outside church walls to the LGBTQI community and everywhere else they find themselves (Lonnie Frisbee – Gay Vessel).

How will the church respond?

"I want to go to the people that Lonnie went to," says David Di Sabatino, "and that would be the disenfranchised." The premise of his highly recommended documentary film is, "'If God can use this guy, then you're all invited.' And the ironic thing is that the face of God on earth, the Church, is turning people away because they're not up to snuff. I think we need to revisit that" (Chattaway).

Baldock has heard from those in the traditional church, "There is no such thing as a gay (or trans) Christian." Her reply? "Well, fellow saints, there is. There are. And more of them are coming back to the God that you have represented as hating and rejecting them" (Baldock, Uncomfortable).

Matthew Vines agrees. "The question is not whether gay Christians exist. It's simply *How will the church respond to them?*" (Vines 40)

God can use LGBTQIs

Rainbow Harvest exhorts gay Christians with these words:

> Lonnie Frisbee was only free when he died, for in death, he returned to God who accepted him. **Our freedom in Christ is intrinsically linked to our freedom of accepting our sexual orientation.** If we [are] unable to accept that God loves us and accepts us, including our sexual orientation, how can we accept Him as our Lord and Savior?
>
> **If we want the Holy Spirit to work mightily through us, then we must come to a point of grace, a point of faith, that we are clean and holy vessels where the Spirit of God can flow mightily, as opposed to considering ourselves as**

sinners or of a fallen nature because we're gay. (Lonnie Frisbee – Gay Vessel, emphasis mine)

Evangelical author Justin Lee confesses that he spent years thinking something was wrong with him because he was gay. He was convinced that in order for God to use him, he would have to become straight.

"I now realize God's been able to use me even more because I'm gay. In a culture that sees gays and Christians as enemies, **gay Christians are in a unique position to bring peace and change minds**" (Lee 243, emphasis mine).

If LGBTQI people receive the message of unconditional love, acceptance, and complete inclusion in Christ, they'll not only pull up their chairs to the Kingdom table, they'll be over-joyed to invite others also. They'll enrich the church with their gifts. They'll go out to the highways and hedges in the power of the Spirit to bring in the lost.

Rev. Samuel Kader declares, "It has too long been assumed a person could not be gay and Christian. But too many gay people have experienced a genuine encounter with the Holy Spirit through faith in Christ to accept this fallacy any longer" (Kader 10).

Yet gays and even gay Christians are still experiencing rejection and hostility from the non-affirming church. Lee claims in *Torn*, "If Christians in our culture are killing Christianity, the gay Christians just might be the ones who are able to save it" (Lee 244). He says,

God wants to use gay Christians—along with bi Christians, and trans Christians, and others in similar situations—to help the church become what she's supposed to be. That means that **we who are gay and Christian must accept the calling and take our place in the church,** working in the various ways we're led to make the world and the church a better place. It also means that **straight Christians must work to ensure that gay Christians are welcomed and supported at all levels of the church,** and that their unique experiences and insight are honored. (244, emphasis mine)

32. Queer Revival

Although some traditional mainline denominations are affirming to gays and lesbians, most churches that are Pentecostal or charismatic are not. In fact, they're vehemently opposed to gay rights.

Anthony Heilbut points out that "Pentecostals, and more particularly black Pentecostal churches... emphasize two themes: prosperity gospel and opposition to gay rights" (Harrison).

All flesh

This leaves LGBTQI believers in dry places. Social action is a good thing, but it's the Spirit of life in Christ Jesus that sets people free (Rom. 8:2). It's the Holy Spirit who empowers for service and draws the lost into the Kingdom of God as on the Day of Pentecost.

> Peter replied, "Each of you must repent of your sins and turn to God, and be baptized in the name of Jesus Christ for the forgiveness of your sins. Then you will receive the gift of the Holy Spirit. This promise is to you, to your children, *and to those far away—all who have been called by the Lord our God."*
> —ACTS 2:38–39 NLT

This promise is for "those far away"—not from the heart of God, but from the heart of the church. All means all, including LGBTQIs. Says Kader: "Gay people and other sexual minorities *are* being empowered with the Holy Spirit and living a Spirit-led life" (Kader 208).

"Most centrally, the Christian community is a witness to the message of redemption," proclaims Mark Yarhouse. "Redemption is not found by measuring how well a person's gender identity aligns with their biological sex, but by drawing them to the person and work of Jesus Christ, and to the power of the Holy Spirit to transform us into his image" (Yarhouse).

Is there anyone for whom Jesus did not die? The Apostle Paul declares, "For God was in Christ, reconciling *the world* to himself, no longer counting people's sins against them. And he gave us this wonderful message of reconciliation. ... God has given us this task of reconciling people to him" (2 Cor. 5:19,18 NLT).

All are included in Christ's sacrifice. God is *already reconciled* with all people of any orientation (Rom. 5:10). And he has charged us with the responsibility of communicating this good news to those we can reach.

The last thing the risen Jesus said before he ascended to heaven to claim the throne of his Kingdom was,

> "I have been given all authority in heaven and on earth. Therefore, go and make disciples of all the nations, baptizing them in the name of the Father and the Son and the Holy Spirit. Teach these new disciples to obey all the commands I have given you. And be sure of this: I am with you always, even to the end of the age."
> —*MATTHEW 28:18–20 NLT*

To fulfill the Great Commission, the straight church must not only accept LGBTQI people, who are no worse sinners than they were, but they must equip them to reach the people only they can reach. To do this, LGBTQI believers need to be clothed with power from on high (Luke 24:49). They need the Pentecostal power that Lonnie Frisbee walked in. They need the authority of Jesus and the anointing of the Holy Spirit to proclaim the good news with signs and wonders following (Luke 4:18–19). Baldock shares that

> God is doing deep spiritual things in the gay, lesbian, bisexual and transgender community. **I believe there is a "revival" and spiritual awakening coming to the gay and trans community.** This is a blasphemous thought to some; every revival has been discounted by the "religious" at the onset and, no doubt, this one may be seen as such as it unfolds. (Baldock, Uncomfortable, emphasis mine)

The first-century church balked at the inclusion of the Gentiles (Acts 11:1–18). The church at the beginning of the twentieth century was scandalized by the Pentecostal outpouring of the Spirit not simply because of spiritual manifestations but because whites worshiped together with blacks.[30] Yet, according to the writings of Paul, *these divisions must dissolve in the all-inclusive Body of Christ.*[31]

---

30 See http://www.christianitytoday.com/gleanings/2014/february/black-and-white-pentecostals-mend-assemblies-of-god-upcag.html.

31 See John 10:16; Acts 2:17, 21; 10:34–35; Romans 3:22; 10:12; 1 Corinthians 12:13; Galatians 3:28; Colossians 3:11.

What about AIDS?

Many Christians have trouble accepting that God loves the LGBTQI community because of HIV and AIDS. Some actually consider the advent of AIDS to be God's judgment against gays. Christian philosopher Philip Yancy warns us about this attitude.

> "Vengeance is mine," God said, and whenever we mortals try to appropriate His vengeance, we tread on dangerous ground. Among the gays in my neighborhood, Christians' statements about the AIDS crisis have done little to encourage repentance. Judgment without love makes enemies, not converts (Yancy 64).

Former U.S. Surgeon General C. Everett Koop stated in the introductory statement to his 1986 *Report on AIDS*, "We are fighting a disease—not people" (Koop).

HIV is not a "gay disease," it's a blood-borne human disease. In 2011 the World Health Organization identified HIV/AIDS as the seventh leading cause of death among *women* (Women's Health).

Barbara Johnson maintains that AIDS plays no favorites. "AIDS has changed our lives forever and we must reach out to each other. As never before, we realize we are marching relentlessly toward the grave. Truly life IS a sexually transmitted, terminal disease" (Johnson 125, 128).

Someone Jesus loves has AIDS. When asked whether an estranged child who has developed the syndrome should be allowed to come home, Johnson asks, *What would Jesus do?* "Wouldn't He care for the sick and injured and the dying?

Wouldn't He bring healing and comfort to those in distress for WHATEVER reason?" (126)

Jesus did not come to judge the world, but to *save* it (John 12:47). This word "save" is *sozo* in Greek, which means not only to deliver spiritually, but to rescue from danger or destruction, and to *heal those suffering of disease.*[32] "He didn't come to bring AIDS," declares Kader, "He came to bring salvation" (Kader 12).

Baldock reminds us, from a personal interview with counselor and priest D. Greg Smith, "Our job as Christians is to jump into another's suffering and work to alleviate it, not walk by on the opposite side of the road" (Baldock, Walking the Bridgeless Canyon 177).

Baldock poses the question, *What if AIDS was not God's penalty, but evil's threat for destruction, again?*

> The Christian church had a mission field millions-huge to go and love on, yet we finger-pointed and cursed. We let AIDS victims die alone and shamed. **Who will ever know how many anointed people of God—the ones who do the full-body lean on Him—died?** (Baldock, Uncomfortable, emphasis mine)

Lonnie Frisbee was one of them. Despite his mistakes, he depended on God, who used him to pour out the Holy Spirit on both the lost and the found of his generation. **Lonnie was a catalyst for revival in the Jesus Movement, and he's a catalyst for the new move of the Holy Spirit among the outcasts of this generation.**

---

32 Strong's G4982.

Revival is coming to the LGBTQI community

Because of Christ's substitutionary work for all people,[33] God can pour out his Spirit on all flesh.[34] Revival *can* and *is* coming to LGBTQIs. In "The Rise of Gay Evangelical Charismatics," Rainbow Harvest shares some inspiring and exciting thoughts about revival.

> [T]he Holy Spirit has been bringing REVIVAL through the new wave of Modern Protestantism in the last 50 years and this move of God is now spreading to the GLBT community.
>
> It appears that the revival... is taking upon a more charismatic and evangelical tone to the disdain of many progressives, seeing it as abandoning liberal theological integrity. **Ironically, those who move by the Holy Spirit of God should have been the first to discern the acceptance of God of the GLBT community.**
>
> There is a rethinking of theology focusing on the grace of God in Christ Jesus rather than the religious laws, which [have] become a bondage. Without the Holy Spirit of God, it is difficult to live out the ministry of Christ with grace or interpret the Bible consistently for our modern times/context. The grace of God is not really a teaching, but it is Christ the person. The churches are moving to a greater understanding of God's grace, the heart of God, which will eventually include the GLBT community. (Rise of Gay Evangelical Charismatics, emphasis mine)

---

33 Romans 5:6, 10, 15, 18–19.

34 Joel 2:28–32; Acts 2:16–22, 38–39.

A fresh vision of grace and radical inclusion is being preached by those like Thomas F. Torrance in *The Mediation of Christ* and Jeff Turner in *Saints in the Arms of a Happy God.* (See "Appendix: Recommended Resources" on page 199.)

Kader asserts, "The revival that comes through the eunuch community in Isaiah 56:5 happens within God's house. God does not have two kinds of churches, 'them and us.' There is only one body" (Kader 137). "God declares that all shall be brought to *God's house.* If God intends to bring them in, who can stop Him?" (138)

As LGBTQI believers come out, claim their unique identity, and walk by faith in Christ, they will experience the coming move of the Spirit. Rainbow Harvest testifies:

It was the Holy Spirit of God whose still and quiet voice confronted me that I was gay. I already knew. God was asking me to accept my own sexual orientation. I was the problem and not God, because I wanted to belong, and being gay would mean being an outcast. **Being gay and Christian broke through all my self-righteousness and pride. God knew, and God had accepted me. Who am I to reject myself when God already had accepted my sexuality? I was accepted in the beloved, accepted in Jesus Christ.**

There is a wind blowing, a mighty wind; it is the Holy Spirit of God moving amongst gay charismatic evangelical Christians to come out.

…God is doing a mighty move this day. **New GLBT churches are arising in the US and Asia that will move in the mighty power of the Holy Spirit by God's love, grace**

and mercy.[35] **They will be praising God aloud with tongues, filled with the Holy Spirit of God. ...**

God's amazing grace is coming. (Rise of Gay Evangelical Charismatics, emphasis mine)

Rev. Elaine Sundby, founder of Faith Full Gospel Church, declares that revival *is* happening, and it's happening "in a place and with a people that most in the Church [have] labeled an abomination" (Sundby 173).

Kathy Baldock proclaims, "If you stand in the way of this move of God, prepare to be knocked down."

What happened among the hippies in the Jesus People movement is happening again in the LGBTQI community because "God has never needed the permission of the Church to act and move in the Spirit" (Baldock, Uncomfortable).

Kader encourages with these words:

Everyone who feels disenfranchised, or feels like they just don't fit in and can't worship together with the rest, God will restore. God will gather them. ... **When God promises to bring restoration to the church, all the things we see in the early church can be expected to be restored....** (Kader 139, emphasis mine)

Accepted in the Beloved

Lonnie Frisbee was anointed by God to reach the lost in his generation. But his ministry was cut short by lack of accep-

---

35 Visit http://www.gaychurch.org/.

tance—firstly of himself, and then by those who rejected him because he was gay.

What would have happened if he had come to terms with his orientation and lived a healthy life, accepted by his peers?

An estimated 3.5% of the United States identifies as LGBT (LGBT Demographics of the U.S.). As of December 2, 2015, the United States has a total resident population of 322,267,564 (Demographics of the U.S.). This means there are *11.3 million Americans who are gay, lesbian, bisexual, or transgender.*

What if the church reached out to them in love, without judgment, and led them to the cross, where they were included in Christ's suffering? What then if they ran to the empty tomb, where they were included in eternal life? What if they were baptized, empowered by the Holy Spirit, and discipled to share their faith?

What would happen if those gay apostles, prophets, evangelists, pastors, and teachers waiting in the wings realized they are forgiven by God and accepted in the Beloved? What if they received the fullness of the Holy Spirit and were encouraged to walk in their calling and anointing to reach the LGBTQI community and the world? What would happen?

We would see another revival like the Jesus Movement. We would be that much closer to the final harvest, the return of Christ, and the establishment of his Kingdom over the nations.

One more question:

What if you came out of the closet and accepted who you are, faults and all, and prayed, "Christ, come into my heart… Oh, Lord, *use* me. Use *me* to reach the world for Jesus"?

The revival will have begun.

Send the Spirit now, for Jesus Christ's sake. Send the Spirit now powerfully, for Jesus Christ's sake. Send the Spirit now more powerfully, for Jesus Christ's sake. Send the Spirit now still more powerfully, for Jesus Christ's sake.

—*Evan Roberts, 1904*

Appendix: Golden Gate Opens in San Francisco, Impacts the World

Doug Addison is a prominent international conference speaker, author, and has been a featured guest on television and radio for a number of years. His events are fun and high-energy as he uses media and stand-up comedy as a means of communicating deep insights. He's an experienced prophetic dream interpreter and a professional stand-up comedian. Visit www.dougaddison.com for more information.

I'm including this prophecy here because I feel it speaks of revival coming not only to the West Coast, but to the LGBTQI community.

Prophetic Word for San Francisco and the West Coast

Doug Addison
December 15, 2011[36]

I have had a series of spiritual experiences and prophetic dreams that are all very positive and are intended to bring hope and encouragement. Although this prophetic word is centered on San Francisco and the West Coast, what is about to happen will impact the entire world.

---

36 http://dougaddison.com/2011/12/golden-gate-opens-in-san-francsico-impacts-the-world/

New Move of God Coming to San Francisco

On 11/11/11 I had a dream that a strong spiritual wind was blowing from Southern California to the north. In my dream most people were not aware that this time of refreshing was already happening in the spirit. Then without warning, the wind suddenly shifted and began to blow from north to south. The wind of the Spirit was now coming from San Francisco to impact Southern California. End of dream.

This change of wind direction is similar to how the last revival in the U.S. started. In 1971, The Jesus People Movement with Lonnie Frisbee started in San Francisco and moved south to Southern California and then impacted the world.

I have been having a lot of dreams and spiritual experiences regarding **a new move of God coming to the West Coast of the U.S. like a huge spiritual wave or wind**. It will first impact San Francisco and then the world. From November 17–20 my wife and I were ministering in the San Francisco Bay Area and God gave me the go-ahead to release these prophetic words. This meeting was one of my more powerful experiences. Something opened in the Heavens. You can listen to it on my podcast. Click on "Prophetic Word for San Francisco and the West Coast": http://dougaddison.com/podcast.

God showed me that many people have been watching and waiting for God's judgment against San Francisco. Some have prayed Psalm 56:7: "Because of their wickedness do not let them escape; in your anger, God, bring the nations down."

But God says that He has indeed found some that have prayed and cried out on behalf of San Francisco and the West Coast. These intercessors have been literally crying and claiming Psalm 56:8–9, "Record my misery; list my tears on your scroll—are they not in your record? Then my enemies will turn back when I call for help. By this I will know that God is for me."

Tears in a Bottle

On November 17 when I arrived to the first session of the San Francisco Bay Area meetings, there was a mist falling over the building. I felt the mist was God's tears being shed over His people in the area. That night I had an open vision of a man weeping over San Francisco. An angel was standing in front of the man capturing his tears in a bottle. When the angel touched the bottle the tears turned into one drop of liquid gold from Heaven. The angel poured the liquid anointing onto San Francisco and the surrounding area.

There have been people crying out to God, but the enemy has made them think that God has forgotten their tears. God has not forgotten, and there will be a great change happening shortly. What I saw about the tears, though centered in San Francisco, it is also happening in other cities around the world.

I was one of those intercessors from 1988–1998 that literally cried over San Francisco. There were times when it seemed hopeless to reach this city that is loved by God. But, "Those who sow in tears will reap with songs of joy," Psalm 126:5.

Wave of the Spirit Hits San Francisco Bay Area

A golden gate is opening in San Francisco! I have had several dreams over the past couple of months in which I have seen a big wave of the Spirit hitting the San Francisco Bay Area. One of the waves hit Candlestick Park (49ers football stadium).

God said that as a result of this new move, San Francisco would become "a candlestick of light for the world to see." Watch and wait with expectation because God will be releasing new things on a greater level after March 4, 2012.

Angel Is Ready to Dance

I had a spiritual experience at Rosh Hashanah (September 28th) in which I saw an angel that was in position and about to dance. I was shown that when this angel dances it will shake things open and release finances, favor and an anointing to bring people into God's Kingdom. In the experience, we all waited with anticipation and the angel danced, and the ground shook and golden coins filled the streets. This is symbolic of Kingdom finances that will be needed to impact the world for God. This included the media, high-tech and entertainment industries. In the vision the place I saw the angel standing looked like a combination of San Francisco, Las Vegas, and Hollywood. These are places that have the appearance of evil but God wants to use them to impact the world.

A Sign from Heaven

I am always cautious about giving prophetic words of a larger magnitude as many people have been suffering from prophetic disappointments. Hope deferred can make your heart sick (Proverbs 13:12). So at the end of the San Francisco meetings, I asked God to give us a sign that we would know He is with us (Psalm 86:17). The next day as we drove south on Highway 101 from San Francisco, a bright rainbow literally followed to the left of our car for several hours. Then as we entered King City, CA, it turned into one of the most brilliant full double rainbows we have ever seen. It was significant that it was a double-rainbow over "King City" as God is making a covenant to bring a double blessing to the Kingdom.

Angels of Strength and Preparation

On November 27th, I felt the presence of angels in my house, but they were different from those normally around me. An angel spoke to me Ephesians 3:16, "I pray that out of His glorious riches He may strengthen you with power through his Spirit in your inner being." It was obvious the angels had come to give strength and to prepare for what lies ahead. This is happening to many people everywhere right now. Trust that you are being prepared and strengthened.

Be Prepared and Don't Get Distracted

I believe that much of what I am seeing from God is very symbolic and the new move coming to the San Francisco area will impact the entire West Coast, Hollywood, and the world. It's time to cry out for our cities everywhere, asking God to pour out His power and love and to have mercy over judgment. That being said, it is possible that there might be earthquakes, but that comes with living on a fault-line. We should all be prepared and have extra food and water on hand no matter where we live. And most of all, do not be afraid.

In many of the experiences I had, there were a great deal of people who had become so distracted with their own life situations that they missed the day of visitation. Do not get distracted away from God's greater purposes. Ask God to give you "eyes to see" into each situation that happens to you.

God is passionately in love with you and people everywhere. This truly is an amazing time to be alive. Get ready for things to shake open and take off in 2012.

Blessings,

Doug Addison
InLight Connection
www.dougaddison.com (Addison)

Appendix: Recommended Resources

The following resources are recommended for further study and enjoyment. The list is divided between print, Internet, and video.

Print

Baldock, Kathy. *Walking the Bridgeless Canyon: Repairing the Breach Between the Church and the LGBT Community*. Reno, NV: Canyonwalker Press, 2014. Print. ISBN 9781619200289.

Brownson, James V. *Bible, Gender, Sexuality: Reframing the Church's Debate on Same-Sex Relationships*. Grand Rapids, MI: William B. Eerdmans Publishing Company, 2013. Print. ISBN 0802868630.

Buckingham, Jamie. *Daughter of Destiny: Kathryn Kuhlman*. Alachua, FL: Bridge-Logos Publishing, 1999. Print. ISBN 0882707841.

Cottrell, Susan. *Mom, I'm Gay: Loving Your LGBTQ Child Without Sacrificing Your Faith*. Austin, TX: FreedHearts.org, 2014. Print. ISBN 162903021X.

Crowder, John. *Cosmos Reborn*. Marylhurst, OR: Sons of Thunder Ministries & Publications, 2013. Print. ISBN 0977082636.

Crowder, John. *Mystical Union*. Marylhurst, OR: Sons of
    Thunder Ministries & Publications, 2010. Print. ISBN
    097708261X.

Enroth, Ronald, Edward E. Ericonson Jr., and C. Breckinridge
    Peters. *The Jesus People: Old-Time Religion in the Age of
    Aquarius*. Grand Rapids, MI: William B. Eerdmans
    Publishing Company, 1972. Print. ISBN 0802814433.

Epstein, Daniel Mark. *Sister Aimee: The Life of Aimee Semple
    McPherson*. San Diego, CA: Harcourt Brace & Company,
    1994. Print. ISBN 0156000938.

Eskridge, Larry. *God's Forever Family: The Jesus People
    Movement in America*. Oxford, UK: Oxford University Press.
    2013. Print. ISBN 9780195326451.

Frisbee, Lonnie, and Roger Sachs. *Not By Might Nor By Power:
    The Jesus Revolution*. Santa Maria, CA: Freedom
    Publications, 2012. Print. ISBN 0978543319.

Howard, Lee Allen. *Response to a Concerned Heterosexual
    Christian*. Jamestown, NY: Acceptable Books, 2012. Print:
    ISBN 978-0692529881; Kindle: ASIN B006UZ7GPG.

Howard, Lee Allen. *The Sin of Sodom: What the Bible Really
    Teaches about Why God Destroyed the Cities of the Plain*.
    Jamestown, NY: Accepted in the Beloved Books, 2015. Print:
    ISBN 978-0692529690.

Jackson, Bill. *The Quest for the Radical Middle: A History of the
    Vineyard*. Capetown, South Africa: Vineyard International
    Publishing, 1999. Print. ISBN 0620243198.

Kader, Samuel. *Openly Gay, Openly Christian: How the Bible Really Is Gay Friendly*. Grapevine, TX: SEGR Publishing LLC, 2013. Print. ISBN 161920021X.

Lee, Justin. *Torn: Rescuing the Gospel from the Gays-vs.-Christians Debate*. New York, NY: Jericho Books, 2012. Print. ISBN 9781455514304.

Perry, Troy. *The Lord Is My Shepherd and He Knows I'm Gay*. Los Angeles, CA: Universal Fellowship Press, 1972. Print.

Philpott, Kent. *Memoirs of a Jesus Freak*. San Rafael, CA: Earthen Vessel Publishing, 2014. Print. ISBN 9780989804110.

Salazar, Lisa. *Transparently: Behind the Scenes of a Good Life*. Self-published, 2011. Print. ISBN 098693190X.

Smith, Chuck, and Hugh Steven. *The Reproducers: New Life for Thousands*. Philadelphia, PA: Calvary Chapel of Philadelphia, 2011. Print. ISBN 0983595003.

Sundby, Elaine T. *Calling the Rainbow Nation Home: A Story of Acceptance and Affirmation*. Lincoln, NE: iUniverse, 2005. Print. ISBN 0595336299.

Torrance, Thomas F. *The Mediation of Christ*. Helmers & Howard Publishers. Print. ISBN 0939443503.

VanderWal-Gritter, Wendy. *Generous Spaciousness: Responding to Gay Christians in the Church*. Grand Rapids, MI: Brazos Press, 2014. Print. ISBN 1587433559.

Vines, Matthew. *God and the Gay Christian: The Biblical Case in Support of Same-Sex Relationships*. New York, NY: Convergent Books, 2014. Print. ISBN 9781601425164.

White, Mel. *Stranger at the Gate: To Be Gay and Christian in America*. New York, NY: Plume, 1994. Print.

Internet

"An Exclusive Interview with the Director of Frisbee: The Life and Death of a Hippie Preacher." ChristianNightmares.tumblr.com. Web. 2014 <http://christiannightmares.tumblr.com/post/64657227995/an-exclusive-interview-with-the-director-of>.

"Frisbee: The Life and Death of a Hippie Preacher." KQED Arts Department. KQED Inc. Web. 19 Nov. 2006. <http://www.kqed.org/arts/programs/trulyca/episode.jsp?epid=152173>.

"LGBT-Sexual Orientation." American Psychiatric Association. Web. <http://www.psychiatry.org/mental-health/people/lgbt-sexual-orientation>.

"Lonnie Frisbee – A Gay Vessel for the Holy Spirit." *Rainbow Harvest* (Psa91.com). Web. Date unknown. <http://psa91.com/frisbee.htm>.

"Lonnie Frisbee Memorial Service," parts 1–8. Vine & Branches Television. 10 Oct. 2010. Web. <https://www.youtube.com/watch?v=8eQ7p6pjq7s>.

"Lonnie Frisbee, Mother's Day, 1980" parts 1–5. Vine & Branches Television. 04 Jan. 2011. Web. <https://www.youtube.com/watch?v=hYVEOJt1op4&list=PLZPvyXXAhiCVbp0KSL7W2B-LnssuHXxlH>.

"A Room of Ex-Gay Survivors Reacts to Alan Chambers' Apology." *Our America with Lisa Ling*/OWN TV. Web. 20

June 2013. <https://www.youtube.com/
watch?v=x0SZC3Azsqw>.

"The Roots: Lonnie Frisbee." <http://www.inplainsite.org/html/
vineyard_lonnie_frisbee.html>.

AIDS Interfaith Network. <http://
www.aidsinterfaithnetwork.org/.

American Psychological Association. "Appropriate Therapeutic
Responses to Sexual Orientation." 2009. Web (PDF). <http://
www.apa.org/pi/lgbt/resources/therapeutic-response.pdf>.

Baldock, Kathy. "The (Un)comfortable Spiritual Blessings and
Prophecy on Gay and Trans Christians." Canyonwalker
Connections. Web. Date unknown. http://
canyonwalkerconnections.com/the-uncomfortable-spiritual-
blessing-and-prophecy-on-gay-and-trans-christians/>.

Beyond ExGay: An online community for those who have
survived ex-gay experiences. <http://beyondexgay.com/>.

Billiter, Bill. "GARDEN GROVE: Funeral Services for 'Hippie
Preacher.'" Los Angeles Times. Web. 18 March 1993. <http://
articles.latimes.com/1993-03-18/local/me-12297_1_hippie-
preacher>.

Campolo, Tony. "Tony Campolo: For the Record."
TonyCampolo.org. Web. 08 June 2015. <http://
tonycampolo.org/for-the-record-tony-campolo-releases-a-
new-statement/#.VXd2V0YR9hw>.

Chattaway, Peter T. "Documentary of a Hippie Preacher."
Christianity Today. Web. 19 Apr. 2005. <http://
www.christianitytoday.com/ct/2005/aprilweb-only/
daviddisabatino.html>.

Coker, Matt. "Ears on Their Head, But They Don't Hear: Spreading the Real Message of Frisbee." *OC Weekly*. Web. 14 Apr 2005. <http://www.ocweekly.com/2005-04-14/film/ears-on-their-heads-but-they-don-t-hear/full/>.

Coker, Matt. "The First Jesus Freak." *OC Weekly*. Web. 03 Mar. 2005. http://www.ocweekly.com/content/printVersion/42509/>.

Cooperman, Alan. "Minister Admits to Buying Drugs and Massage." *Washington Post*. Web. 4 Nov. 2006. <http://www.washingtonpost.com/wp-dyn/content/article/2006/11/03/AR2006110301617.html.

"Copy of The Holy Family By Lonnie Frisbee Evangelist, Prophet, Apostle." *YouTube*. Web. 06 Sept. 2015. <https://www.youtube.com/watch?v=HsANDQgRVSM>

Family Acceptance Project. <http://familyproject.sfsu.edu/>.

Ford, Zack. "What Was Missing from an Ex-Gay Leader's Apology." *ThinkProgress.org*. Web. 24 July 2013. <http://thinkprogress.org/lgbt/2013/07/24/2350401/what-was-missing-from-an-ex-gay-leaders-apology/>.

Gartner, Richard B., PhD., "Talking about Sexually Abused Boys, and the Men They Become." *Psychology Today*. Web. 30 Jan. 2011. <https://www.psychologytoday.com/blog/psychoanalysis-30/201101/talking-about-sexually-abused-boys-and-the-men-they-become>.

Gay Christian Network (Justin Lee). <http://www.gaychristian.net/>.

GayChurch.org. <http://www.gaychurch.org/>.

Intersex Society of North America. <http://www.isna.org/>.

Lonnie Frisbee Facebook page. <https://www.facebook.com/lonnierayfrisbee>.

Mathias, Anita. "Lonnie Frisbee, the Most Influential Gay Christian in the Last Century." Web. 25 Aug. 2012. <http://anitamathias.com/2012/08/25/lonnie-frisbee-the-most-influential-gay-christian-in-the-last-century/>

Metropolitan Community Churches (Troy Perry). <http://mccchurch.org/>.

"Painting of Abraham and Son by Artist Lonnie Frisbee." *YouTube.* Web. 06 Sept. 2015. <https://www.youtube.com/watch?t=13&v=NyRc_IlbPtE>

"Painting of the Easter Morning Tomb by Artist Lonnie Frisbee." *YouTube.* Web. 06 Sept. 2015. <https://www.youtube.com/watch?v=NOx6qaGaXsQ>

Reformation Project (Matthew Vines). <http://www.reformationproject.org/>.

Schlanger, Zoë, and Elijah Wolfson. "Ex-Ex-Gay Pride." *Newsweek.* Web. 1 May 2014. <http://www.newsweek.com/ex-ex-gay-pride-249282>.

Soulforce (Mel White). <http://www.soulforce.org/>.

Yarhouse, Mark. "Understanding the Transgender Phenomenon." *Christianity Today.* Web. 08 June 2015. <http://www.christianitytoday.com/ct/2015/july-august/understanding-transgender-gender-dysphoria.html>.

Video

Call Me Troy. Dir. Bloom, Scott. 2007. DVD. Tragoidia Moving Pictures. <http://www.amazon.com/Call-Me-Troy-Scott-Bloom/dp/B006G2FTNY/>

Frisbee: The Life and Death of a Hippie Preacher. Dir. Di Sabatino, David. 2005. DVD. Jester Media. <http://fallenangeldoc.com/store.html>

The Jesus People. 1972. Video. Pyramid Films. <https://www.youtube.com/watch?v=XmUvnN3mtuc>.

The Keith Green Story: Your Love Broke Through. Dir. Daren Thomas. 2002. Video. Sparrow Records. <https://www.youtube.com/watch?v=fXOhSScVMUs>.

Through My Eyes. Dir. Justin Lee. 2009. DVD. The Gay Christian Network. <https://www.gaychristian.net/store/through-my-eyes-dvd>.

Works Cited

Addison, Doug. "Golden Gate Opens in San Francisco: Impacts the World." 14 Dec. 2011. *DougAddison.com*. Web. 23 June 2015. <http://dougaddison.com/2011/12/golden-gate-opens-in-san-francsico-impacts-the-world/>.

Ahn, Ché. *Spirit-Led Evangelism*. Grand Rapids, MI: Chosen Books, 2006. Print.

American Psychiatric Association. "LGBT Sexual Orientation." n.d. *Psychiatry.org*. Web. 20 May 2015. <http://www.psychiatry.org/mental-health/people/lgbt-sexual-orientation>.

"Association of Vineyard Churches." 21 May 2015. *Wikipedia.org*. Web. 23 June 2015. <https://en.wikipedia.org/wiki/Association_of_Vineyard_Churches>.

Baldock, Kathy. "Uncomfortable Spiritual Blessings and Prophecy on Gay and Trans Christians, The." n.d. *CanyonwalkerConnections.com*. Web. 22 May 2015. <http://canyonwalkerconnections.com/the-uncomfortable-spiritual-blessing-and-prophecy-on-gay-and-trans-christians/>.

—. *Walking the Bridgeless Canyon: Repairing the Breach Between the Church and the LGBT Community*. Reno, NV: Canyonwalker Press, 2014. Print.

Billiter, Bill. "GARDEN GROVE: Funeral Services for 'Hippie Preacher'." 18 Mar. 1993. *LATimes.com*. Web. 10 May 2015.

<http://articles.latimes.com/1993-03-18/local/me-12297_1_hippie-preacher>.

Browning, Kari. "Lonnie Frisbee, 'Hippie Preacher'." n.d. *Identity Network.* Web. 09 May 2015. <http://www.identitynetwork.net/apps/articles/?articleid=77983&columnid=2093>.

Butcher, Andy. "Roberts Liardon Steps Down." 31 Jan. 2002. *CharismaMag.com.* Web. 20 May 2015. <http://www.charismamag.com/site-archives/134-peopleevents/people-events/554-roberts-liardon-steps-down>.

"Calvary Chapel." 12 June 2015. *Wikipedia.org.* Web. 23 June 2015. <https://en.wikipedia.org/wiki/Calvary_Chapel>.

Campolo, Tony. "Tony Campolo: For the Record." 08 June 2015. *TonyCampolo.org.* Web. 09 June 2015. <http://tonycampolo.org/for-the-record-tony-campolo-releases-a-new-statement/#.VXd2V0YR9hw>.

Cauchi, Tony. "Charles Fox Parham." 2004. *Revival-Library.org.* Web. 25 June 2015. <http://www.revival-library.org/pensketches/am_pentecostals/parham.html>.

CBS Reports. "The Homosexuals." 07 Mar. 1967. *Vimeo.com.* Web. 11 June 2015. <https://vimeo.com/61123970>.

Chattaway, Peter T. "Documentary of a Hippie Preacher." 19 Apr. 2005. *ChristianityToday.com.* Web. 09 May 2015. <http://www.christianitytoday.com/ct/2005/aprilweb-only/daviddisabatino.html>.

"Chuck Smith, pastor." 18 May 2015. *Wikipedia.org.* Web. 05 Apr. 2015. <http://en.wikipedia.org/wikiuc/Chuck_Smith_%28pastor%29>.

Coker, Matt. "Ears on Their Head, But They Don't Hear: Spreading the Real Message of Frisbee." 14 Apr. 2005. *OC Weekly*. Web. 07 May 2015. <http://www.ocweekly.com/ 2005-04-14/film/ears-on-their-heads-but-they-don-t-hear/ full/>.

—. "First Jesus Freak, The." 03 Mar. 2005. *OC Weekly*. Web. 05 Apr 2015. <http://www.ocweekly.com/content/printVersion/ 42509/>.

Cooperman, Alan. "Minister Admits to Buying Drugs and Massage." 04 Nov. 2006. *WashingtonPost.com*. Web. 09 June 2015. <http://www.washingtonpost.com/wp-dyn/content/ article/2006/11/03/AR2006110301617.html>.

Crouch, Andy. "Sex Without Bodies." 26 June 2013. *ChristianityToday.com*. Web. 09 June 2015. <http:// www.christianitytoday.com/ct/2013/july-august/sex-without-bodies.html>.

Crowder, Hardin. "Forgotten Hippy: Remembering Lonnie Frisbee and the Jesus Movement, The." 12 Mar. 2013. *Benevolent Baptist*. Web. 21 May 2015. <https:// benevolentbaptist.wordpress.com/2013/03/12/the-forgotten-hippy-remembering-lonnie-frisbee-and-the-jesus-movement/>.

"Demographics of the United States." 09 June 2015. *Wikipedia.org*. Web. 20 June 2015. <http://en.wikipedia.org/ wiki/Demographics_of_the_United_States>.

"Duane Pederson." 03 May 2015. *Wikipedia.org*. Web. 10 May 2015. <http://en.wikipedia.org/wiki/Duane_Pederson>.

Enroth, Ronald, Edward E. Ericson Jr. and C. Breckinridge Peters. *Jesus People: Old-Time Religion in the Age of Aquarius,*

The. Grand Rapids, MI: William B. Eerdmans Publishing
   Company, 1972. Print.

Eskridge, Larry. *God's Forever Family: The Jesus People
   Movement in America*. Oxford, UK: Oxford University Press,
   2013. Print.

"Exclusive Interview with the Director of Frisbee: The Life and
   Death of a Hippie Preacher, An." 2014.
   ChristianNightmares.tumblr.com. Web. 07 June 2015. <http://
   christiannightmares.tumblr.com/post/64657227995/an-
   exclusive-interview-with-the-director-of>.

Frisbee, Lonnie and Roger Sachs. *Not By Might Nor By Power:
   The Jesus Revolution*. Santa Maria, CA: Freedom
   Publications, 2012. Print.

"Frisbee: The Life and Death of a Hippie Preacher." 19 Nov.
   2006. *KQED.org*. Web. 19 May 2015. <http://www.kqed.org/
   arts/programs/trulyca/episode.jsp?epid=152173>.

Frisbee: The Life and Death of a Hippie Preacher. Dir. David
   Di Sabatino. Perf. Lonnie Frisbee. Jester Media. 2006. DVD.

Gartner, Richard B., PhD. "Talking about Sexually Abused Boys,
   and the Men They Become." 30 Jan. 2011.
   PsychologyToday.com. Web. 20 May 2015. <https://
   www.psychologytoday.com/blog/psychoanalysis-30/201101/
   talking-about-sexually-abused-boys-and-the-men-they-
   become>.

Grady, J. Lee. "Prophetic Minister Paul Cain Issues Public
   Apology for Immoral Lifestyle." 28 Feb. 2005.
   CharismaMag.com. Web. 20 May 2015. <http://
   www.charismamag.com/site-archives/154-peopleevents/

people-and-events/1514-prophetic-minister-paul-cain-issues-public-apology-for-immoral-lifestyle->.

"Haggard Admits 'Inappropriate Relationship'." 27 Jan. 2009. *KRDO.com.* Web. 20 June 2015. <http://www.krdo.com/news/Haggard-Admits-Inappropriate-Relationship/1656388>.

Harrison, Douglas. "Gospel Church and the Ruining of Gay Lives: An Interview with Anthony Heilbut, The." 01 Aug. 2012. *ReligionDispatches.org.* Web. 20 May 2015. <http://religiondispatches.org/the-gospel-church-and-the-ruining-of-gay-lives-an-interview-with-anthony-heilbut/>.

"Harvest Christian Fellowship." 30 Nov. 2014. *Wikipedia.org.* Web. 04 Apr. 2015. <http://en.wikipedia.org/wiki/Harvest_Christian_Fellowship>.

Hayward, David. "Lonnie Frisbee, the Church, and Being Gay." 04 Feb. 2010. *Nakedpastor.com.* Web. 09 June 2015. <http://nakedpastor.com/2010/02/lonnie-frisbee-the-church-and-being-gay/>.

Heger, Heinz. *Men with the Pink Triangle: The True Life-and-Death Story of Homosexuals in the Nazi Death Camps, The.* Trans. David Fernbach. Los Angeles, CA: Alyson Publications, Inc., 1994. Print.

Herek, Gregory M. "Facts About Homosexuality and Child Molestation." n.d. *University of California at Davis, Psychology Department (http://psychology.ucdavis.edu/).* Web. 02 Sept. 2015. <http://psychology.ucdavis.edu/faculty_sites/rainbow/html/facts_molestation.html>.

Hinn, Benny. *Anointing, The.* Nashville, TN: Thomas Nelson, Inc., 1997. Print.

"History of the Vineyard Movement." Archived from the original on 15 July 2006. *VineyardUSA.org.* Web. 29 May 2015. <http://web.archive.org/web/20060715183628/http:/ www.vineyardusa.org/ about/history.aspx>.

Jackson, Bill. "A Short History of the Association of Vineyard Churches." Roozen, David A. and James R. Nieman. *Church, Identity, and Change: Theology and Denominational Structures in Unsettled Times.* Grand Rapids: William B. Eerdmans Publishing Company, 2005. Print.

—. *Quest for the Radical Middle: A History of the Vineyard, The.* Capetown, South Africa: Vineyard International Publishing, 1999. Print.

"John Wimber." 29 May 2015. *Wikipedia.org.* Web. 22 June 2015. <https://en.wikipedia.org/wiki/John_Wimber>.

Johnson, Barbara. *Pack Up Your Gloomees in a Great Big Box, Then Sit on the Lid and Laugh!* Dallas, TX: Word Publishing, 1993. Print.

Jones, Tony. "Lonnie Frisbee and the Non-Demise of the Emerging Church." 30 Dec. 2009. *Patheos/Theoblogy.* Web. 09 June 2015. <http://www.patheos.com/blogs/tonyjones/ 2009/12/30/lonnie-frisbee-and-the-non-demise-of-the- emerging-church/>.

Kader, Samuel. *Openly Gay, Openly Christian: How the Bible Really Is Gay Friendly.* Grapevine, TX: SEGR Publishing LLC, 2013. Print.

"Kathryn Kuhlman." 13 May 2015. *Wikipedia.org.* Web. 23 June 2015. <http://en.wikipedia.org/wiki/Kathryn_Kuhlman>.

Kincaid, Timothy. "Newly Refurbished Michael Johnston, The." 17 Jan. 2007. *ExGayWatch.com*. Web. 15 June 2015. <http://exgaywatch.com/2007/01/the-newly-refur/>.

Kinnaman, David and Gabe Lyons. *unChristian: What a New Generation Really Thinks About Christianity… and Why it Matters*. Grand Rapids, MI: Baker Books, 2012. Print.

Koop, C. Everett. "Surgeon General's Report on Acquired Immune Deficiency Syndrome." 22 Oct. 1986. *National Library of Medicine Profiles in Science*. Web (PDF). 12 June 2015. <http://profiles.nlm.nih.gov/NN/B/B/V/N/>.

Kort, Joe. "Homosexuality and Pedophilia: The False Link." 05 Oct. 2012. *HuffingtonPost.com*. Web. 27 June 2015. <http://www.huffingtonpost.com/joe-kort-phd/homosexuality-and-pedophi_b_1932622.html>.

Laurie, Greg and Ellen Vaughn. *Lost Boy*. Ventura, CA: Regal, 2008. Print.

Lee, Justin. *Torn: Rescuing the Gospel from the Gays-vs.-Christians Debate*. New York, NY: Jericho Books, 2012. Print.

"LGBT Demographics of the United States." 20 May 2015. *Wikipedia.org*. Web. 22 May 2015. <http://en.wikipedia.org/wiki/LGBT_demographics_of_the_United_States>.

"Life Pacific College." n.d. *Foursquare.org*. Web. 18 May 2015. <http://www.foursquare.org/leaders/education/life_pacific_college>.

Lloyd-Jones, D. Martyn. *Joy Unspeakable*. Wheaton, IL: Shaw Books, 1984. Print.

"Lonnie Frisbee." 13 Feb. 2006. *As Were Some of You.* Web. 04 Apr. 2015. <https://formerlygay.wordpress.com/2006/02/13/lonnie-frisbee/>.

"Lonnie Frisbee." 04 Apr. 2015. *Wikipedia.org.* Web. 25 Apr. 2015. <https://en.wikipedia.org/wiki/Lonnie_Frisbee>.

"Lonnie Frisbee – A Gay Vessel for the Holy Spirit." n.d. *Rainbow Harvest (Psa91.com).* Web. 04 Apr. 2015. <http://psa91.com/frisbee.htm>.

"Lonnie Frisbee 1993 Memorial Service." 10 Oct. 2010. *YouTube.* Video. 20 June 2015. <https://www.youtube.com/watch?v=zkTRgo0DpvA>.

"Lonnie Frisbee, Mother's Day, 1980." 04 Jan. 2011. *YouTube.* Vine & Branches Television. Video/audio. 13 May 2015. <https://www.youtube.com/watch?v=hYVEOJt1op4&list=PLZPvyXXAhiCVbp0KSL7W2B-LnssuHXxlH>.

Mathias, Anita. "Lonnie Frisbee, the Most Influential Gay Christian in the Last Century." 25 Aug. 2012. *AnitaMathias.com.* Web. 04 Apr. 2015. <http://anitamathias.com/2012/08/25/lonnie-frisbee-the-most-influential-gay-christian-in-the-last-century/>.

Maxwell, Joe. "Laughter Draws Toronto Charismatic Crowds." *Christianity Today.* 24 Oct. 1994: 38. Print.

Moore, S. David. *Shepherding Movement.* New York, NY: T & T Clark International, 2013. Print.

"New Rebel Cry: Jesus is Coming!" *Time.* 21 June 1971. Print.

"Out of the Closet … in the Pulpit of a Megachurch." 14 Nov. 2010. *NPR.org.* Web. 20 May 2015. <http://www.npr.org/

2010/11/14/131312723/out-of-the-closet-in-the-pulpit-of-a-megachurch>.

Perry, Troy D. *Lord Is My Shepherd and He Knows I'm Gay, The.* Los Angeles, CA: Universal Fellowship Press, 1972. Print.

Petrowski, Kenny. "Lonnie Frisbee." 22 Sept. 2006. *Kpetrowski.blogspot.com.* Web. 09 May 2015. <http://kpetrowski.blogspot.com/2006/09/lonnie-frisbee.html>.

Philpott, Kent. *Memoirs of a Jesus Freak.* San Rafael, CA: Earthen Vessel Publishing, 2014. Print.

Richardson, James T. *Regulating Religion: Case Studies from Around the Globe.* New York, NY: Kluwer Academic/Plenum Publishers, 2004. Print.

"Rise of Gay Evangelical Charismatics." n.d. *Rainbow Harvest (Psa91.com).* Web. 04 Apr. 2015. <http://www.psa91.com/evangelicalchrist.htm>.

Robertson, Brandan. "Tony Compolo Calls for Full Inclusion of Gay & Lesbian Christians." 08 June 2015. *Patheos/Revangelical.* Web. 09 June 2015. <http://www.patheos.com/blogs/revangelical/2015/06/08/tony-campolo-comes-out.html>.

Schlanger, Zoë and Elijah Wolfson. "Ex-Ex-Gay Pride." 01 May 2014. *Newsweek.com.* Web. 15 June 2015. <http://www.newsweek.com/ex-ex-gay-pride-249282>.

"Sexual orientation." 17 June 2015. *Wikipedia.org.* Web. 27 June 2015. <https://en.wikipedia.org/wiki/Sexual_orientation>.

"Shepherding Movement." 20 Apr. 2015. *Wikipedia.org.* Web. 20 Apr. 2015. <http://en.wikipedia.org/wiki/Shepherding_Movement>.

Sjogren, Steve. "Lonnie Frisbee Autobiography Coming." 2012. *SteveSjogren.com.* Web. 09 June 2015. <http://www.stevesjogren.com/lonnie-frisbee-autobiography-coming/#.VYlzr0YR9hw>.

Sloane, David. "The People Speak." Nov. 2006. Surfer51.blogspot.com. Web. 06 Sept. 2015.

—. "Shekinah Fellowship." Apr. 2010. Shekinah Fellowship. Web. 06 Sept. 2015.

Smith, Chuck and Hugh Steven. *Reproducers: New Life for Thousands, The.* Philadelphia, PA: Calvary Chapel of Philadelphia, 2011. Print.

Smith, Chuck. *History of Calvary Chapel, The.* Costa Mesa, CA: The Word for Today, n.d. Print.

Stafford, Tim and James Beverley. "Conversations: God's Wonder Worker." 14 July 1997. *ChristianityToday.com.* Web. 13 May 2015. <http://ww.christianitytoday.com/ct/1997/july14/7t8046.html>.

Sundby, Elaine T. *Calling the Rainbow Nation Home: A Story of Acceptance and Affirmation.* Lincoln, NE: iUniverse, 2005. Print.

Synan, Vinson. *Holiness-Pentecostal Tradition: Charismatic Movements in the Twentieth Century, The.* Grand Rapids, MI: William B. Eerdmans Publishing Company, 1997. Print.

Turner, John G. "They Got High on Jesus Instead." 11 July 2013. *ChristianityToday.com.* Web. 07 June 2015. <http://www.christianitytoday.com/ct/2013/july-web-only/gods-forever-family-they-got-high-on-jesus-instead.html>.

Vachon, Brian. *A Time to Be Born*. Englewood Cliffs, NJ: Prentice-Hall Publishers, 1972. Print.

Vines, Matthew. *God and the Gay Christian: The Biblical Case in Support of Same-Sex Relationships*. New York, NY: Convergent Books, 2014. Print.

White, John. *When the Spirit Comes in Power: Signs and Wonders Among God's People*. Downers Grove, IL: InterVarsity Press, 1988. Print.

Wimber, Carol. *John Wimber: The Way It Was*. London, UK: Hodder & Stoughton, 1999. Print.

Wimber, John and Kevin Springer. *Power Evangelism*. San Francisco, CA: Harper & Row, Publishers, 1986. Print.

"Women's Health." Sept. 2013. *World Health Organization (who.int)*. Web. 23 June 2015. <http://www.who.int/mediacentre/factsheets/fs334/en/>.

Yancy, Philip. "Jogging Past the AIDS Clinic." *Christianity Today*. 07 Mar. 1986. Print.

Yarhouse, Mark. "Understanding the Transgender Phenomenon." 08 June 2015. *ChristianityToday.com*. Web. 09 June 2015. <http://www.christianitytoday.com/ct/2015/july-august/understanding-transgender-gender-dysphoria.html>.

Made in the USA
Middletown, DE
04 March 2023

26166280R00137